£4/13
£1.99

SHIFT YOUR THINKING, CHANGE YOUR LIFE

MO SHAPIRO is a Managing Partner of *IN*FORM Training & Communication. She has a proven and outstanding track record as a personal development coach, psychological counsellor, management trainer and public speaker. Mo is a sought-after broadcaster on radio and television. She is the author of four personal development books for the Institute of Management and is on the expert panel of *Real Health and Beauty* magazine, for which she writes regular features. Mo regularly offers her expert advice and coaching input to all popular media. Her mission is to help people achieve their dreams and enjoy them for as long as possible.

G000027009

Overcoming Common Problems Series

For a full list of titles please contact
Sheldon Press, Marylebone Road, London NW1 4DU

The Assertiveness Workbook
A plan for busy women
JOANNA GUTMANN

Birth Over Thirty Five
SHEILA KITZINGER

Body Language
How to read others' thoughts by their
gestures
ALLAN PEASE

Body Language in Relationships
DAVID COHEN

Cancer – A Family Affair
NEVILLE SHONE

Coping Successfully with Hayfever
DR ROBERT YOUNGSON

Coping Successfully with Migraine
SUE DYSON

Coping Successfully with Pain
NEVILLE SHONE

**Coping Successfully with Your Irritable
Bowel**
ROSEMARY NICOL

Coping with Anxiety and Depression
SHIRLEY TRICKETT

Coping with Breast Cancer
DR EADIE HEYDERMAN

Coping with Bronchitis and Emphysema
DR TOM SMITH

Coping with Chronic Fatigue
TRUDIE CHALDER

Coping with Depression and Elation
DR PATRICK McKEON

Curing Arthritis Diet Book
MARGARET HILLS

Curing Arthritis – The Drug-Free Way
MARGARET HILLS

Depression
DR PAUL HAUCK

Divorce and Separation
Every woman's guide to a new life
ANGELA WILLANS

**Everything Parents Should Know About
Drugs**
SARAH LAWSON

Good Stress Guide, The
MARY HARTLEY

Heart Attacks – Prevent and Survive
DR TOM SMITH

Helping Children Cope with Grief
ROSEMARY WELLS

How to Improve Your Confidence
DR KENNETH HAMBLY

How to Interview and Be Interviewed
MICHELE BROWN AND GYLES
BRANDRETH

How to Keep Your Cholesterol in Check
DR ROBERT POVEY

How to Pass Your Driving Test
DONALD RIDLAND

**How to Start a Conversation and Make
Friends**
DON GABOR

How to Write a Successful CV
JOANNA GUTMANN

Hysterectomy
SUZIE HAYMAN

The Irritable Bowel Diet Book
ROSEMARY NICOL

Overcoming Guilt
DR WINDY DRYDEN

The Parkinson's Disease Handbook
DR RICHARD GODWIN-AUSTEN

Talking About Anorexia
How to cope with life without starving
MAROUSHKA MONRO

Think Your Way to Happiness
DR WINDY DRYDEN AND JACK
GORDON

Overcoming Common Problems

SHIFT YOUR THINKING,
CHANGE YOUR LIFE

Mo Shapiro

Published in Great Britain in 2001 by
Sheldon Press
Holy Trinity Church
Marylebone Road
London NW1 4DU

© Mo Shapiro 2001

British Library Cataloguing-in-Publication Data

A catalogue record for this book is available from the British Library

ISBN 085969–854–8

Typeset by Deltatype Limited, Birkenhead, Merseyside
Printed in Great Britain by Biddles Ltd
www.biddles.co.uk

Contents

For Mum and Dad, who've always believed in me

Acknowledgements

There are many people who have contributed directly and indirectly to helping me write *Shift Your Thinking, Change Your Life*.

In particular I would like to thank Liz Marsh at Sheldon Press for asking me to write it and having the confidence that I could. Ali Gunn for her generosity in steering me through matters contractual. Donna Edwards, Emily Chua, Ian MacLaren and Stephanie Holland for being my critical and enthusiastic readers. Jenny Hinds for keeping me and my office in some kind of order during the process. Jo Hodder at the Society of Authors. My family, friends and colleagues who have tolerated my physical and mental absences. The many people I have coached, counselled and trained who have helped me prove that this all works.

My biggest thank you is to Mark Yoxon, whose unconditional support and encouragement have been invaluable. I welcome the opportunity to spend unqualified and fun time with him again.

Introduction

Thank you for choosing to read *Shift Your Thinking, Change Your Life*. However this book has reached you, whether you bought it, were given it or have borrowed it, you have done so because now is the right time for you to be reading it. I know there is something in it especially for you, to help you get to where you want to be. Enjoy the journey and look forward to the changes you want to create.

I have described the sections as 'Shifts', rather than chapters, because they represent movement and activity which give you opportunities to increase the flexibility of your thinking. Some parts of the book will resonate and feel right for you and some bits won't. Feel free to dip in and out as you fancy. Some will immediately provoke a 'yes' reaction, others will take time. You may even buy the book and just skim through it at first. Trust yourself to know when you're ready to go deeper into it.

I have used a number of techniques to generate action into the process. I want to encourage you to be dynamic as well as reading the theories. At various stages I have suggested certain questions you might ask yourself and created some activities to help you delve deeper into your specific understanding and personal relationship to the issues. In some places I have suggested you use your imagination to create things the way you want them to be. You can do this with pictures, words, sounds or just by experiencing the ideas. Whatever works for you is the way to do it. If you record the imagination exercises you can re-use them anytime. You may want to involve some friends and make these social activities, too.

As you journey through the shifts, be aware that you have a choice about what you do with what you read. The more you feel able to exercise choice here, the more you feel enabled to do so in any area of your life. I have used the notion of 'moments of choice' throughout the book. These are there to remind you that if you stop and think, you have more responses available than you might previously have realized. A lot of us make our choices at an unconscious level. The more you bring them into your consciousness, the more empowered you become. You may decide sometimes that you are going to respond to a particular situation with a moan and groan, rather than a straightforward response. This is fine as long as you know that it's your decision and that you understand the effect that the behaviour will have.

I have also made use of many affirmations to reinforce the messages you give yourself about your life. Affirmations are positive, simple and present-tense statements that you can repeat regularly to yourself with the intention of retraining your mind to think in a way you choose, or to change the way you think and therefore the way you act. I sometimes sing mine when I am on a long car journey; other people draw and decorate theirs and hang them around their houses. Repeating positive affirmations can reverse the negativity of the tapes that we play more often in our minds.

As you go through the book you will begin to recognize your 'starters' and 'stoppers'. The more you realize what prevents you from being the you you want to be, or from doing the things you want to do, the greater chance you have to change. In addition, you will acknowledge the ways you motivate yourself and the key ways you get yourself started on projects. Then you can increase the times you bring those into helping you move the way you want. Everyone has examples of some time in their lives when they have got themselves going. With this knowledge you too can go on to repeat your successful strategies in different situations.

This is a play book, not a work book. I want it to be as much fun for you to read and use as writing it has been for me. I have enjoyed researching and reminding myself of the bits that I need to learn about myself and my reactions to life. I know there are days when I need to get a grip of myself, think positively and be grateful that the techniques are there for me. I have plenty of dear friends and acquaintances who are quick to point out when I am living my life along the 'do as I say, not do as I do' lines (not walking the talk). In the main I can laugh and agree; when I can't, and feel myself tensing up, I know they've hit a nerve and identified an area for investigation.

This book is about change, and the only thing that doesn't change about change is change itself. It is often challenging. For some people this means that the sense of achievement felt is greater once the change is successful. There are a number of theories about how long and how many times you need to repeat a new action or behaviour before it becomes part of your make-up.

> It takes three weeks to replace an old habit with a new skill and at least another nine weeks to turn that new skill into a new habit.
>
> (Taylor, 2000)

INTRODUCTION

Please use this book to help you change, and don't use it to beat yourself up if the changes aren't as immediate as you would like. It may be that part of you is resistant because you have become so used to being the way you are – even if you don't like it. It's a familiar and, in an odd way, almost a 'safe' route to take. You know the routine, and the results. How would you feel if you were successful in your change? Perhaps a bit scared at first. Go at your own pace and trust yourself to know that something will happen when you are ready. It may take time. Be kind enough to yourself to take the time to understand yourself and understand why you are the way you are. Give yourself the same time, patience and compassion you would give your best friend if they were in the same place.

Make a commitment to *do* something active, and let the changes begin.

Shift 1
What do you really want?

> The greater danger for most of us is not that our aim is too high and we miss it. But that it is too low ... and we reach it.
>
> (Michelangelo)

Let's begin at the beginning and have some kind of positive end in sight. In my work as a trainer and life coach I spend a lot of time helping people consider and outline the goals they have and want to achieve. In training programmes we start with expectations and objectives for the day and finish with the goals for the future. Well, that's all very easy when you know what you want. It may seem more complicated when you're faced with the thought that you just don't know.

As you read through *Shift Your Thinking, Change Your Life* you may decide that you want to have goals in different areas of your life, and that's great. In fact, it is crucial to set goals for more than one aspect as it provides you with a balance. Some people tend to be familiar with goal and objective setting in a work context, but don't always carry the process through to the rest of their lives. The table on the next page is your chance to do just that and plan for the future you desire.

Take this opportunity to set yourself a mixture of goals that will keep you motivated for some time to come. You can set some that are realistic and that you can imagine achieving, with a bit of effort. Also give yourself some crazy, audacious goals to go for and see what else occurs as you start to put some actions together to go with them. Think about your fantastic, 'beyond dreams' goals. These will really get your energy going and are important to have in mind. Once you start allowing your imagination some daydreaming time, you are likely to have a clearer idea of what you really want.

> You are what you think about all day long.
>
> (Robert Schuller, American evangelist)

Do you have goals in these areas?

		yes	maybe	not yet
Social life	Get out with friends at least once a month			
Relationships	Make time to speak to my partner more often			
Family	Ask for help when I need it			
Finances	Monitor my incomings and outgoings for a month			
Work	Look into options available, crazy ones too			
Living space	Clear out bedroom			
Leisure	Join a choir or local library			
Health	Find someone to exercise with			
Retirement	Collect ideas or start pension			
Spiritual life	Take up meditation			
Contribution	Volunteer for community events			
New habits or releasing old ones	Stop and think before I say 'yes'			
Personal development	Listen to one tape a month			

We know from the autobiographies of people who have succeeded in all walks of life that they dreamt about their eventual outcome regularly and sometimes from an early age. They focused on their goals as almost an obsession. They could picture themselves achieving, hear the acclaim and feel the sense of satisfaction and excitement as they succeeded. Many of them were mocked for having dreams beyond their means, but they believed in themselves and they triumphed. They would notice others who succeeded, too, and where appropriate copy their strategies for success.

Start your goal-setting process assuming that you can succeed. There are no limitations, just go for all the things you'd like to do.

Follow your instincts and practise being there in advance. Before anything you want to happen can occur,

> You must desire that it happen, believe it can happen and expect it to happen.
>
> (Silva and Goldman, 1990)

Imagine

Find a quiet place and give yourself at least 15 minutes to complete the following exercise. You can ask a friend to read it out for you or put it on to an audio cassette so that you can play it any time you want.

Start by concentrating on your breathing and allow yourself to relax into your chair or on the floor if you are lying down.

Enjoy the thought that you are going to release any tension and know that you deserve the time you are giving yourself.

Relax and breathe slowly.

Imagine yourself walking through a wooded area. Notice the trees and flowers, listen to the birds and feel the warm air around you.

As you walk along you come to a clearing with a building in the middle. It seems very welcoming so you go in and wander around.

In the hallway there is an envelope addressed to you; the paper is soft to touch. Open it.

'This is the start of the rest of your life. How would you like to spend it? In Room 1 there is someone you can talk it over with. In Room 2 there are paints and paper, and in Room 3 there are all kinds of objects. Please use all three rooms to help you create your dreams.'

Take as much time as you want to delight in releasing and experiencing all the dreams you've ever had about your life. Imagine being a part of them and enjoy yourself.

When you are ready, leave the building and move back through the wood returning to the place you are in. Be ready to open your eyes, feeling great and inspired. You know you can go back there often and whenever you choose, and keep expanding your options.

I was talking to someone as part of a radio phone-in programme. She wanted to change her job, but wasn't quite sure what to do. Her present job was all right, and she said, 'I quite like doing what I do, but I'm not sure whether to apply for this other job. In the job that I've got now it's very straightforward and it's very easy. But I've seen this other job in the paper and it's what I really want to do – there's something about it that's just me. I'm just not sure whether to apply for it or not.' It was very easy for me to give that person advice. When she talked about the new job, her energy increased, she was much more animated and I think she was grinning as she thought about it. I suggested she go for it and take the chance she was offered. Although she said she wasn't sure, her voice and description sounded certain to me.

It is so important to focus on what you want rather than what you don't want, what you enjoy rather than what you don't enjoy. Consider this. Just stop what you're doing and for 30 seconds, whatever you do, do not think of Donald Duck.

Now be honest, did you see a picture of Donald Duck? Did you hear a little quack? Did you see a beak? Did you hear any sounds or just get a sense of Donald Duck? Maybe you were awkward and you thought about Mickey Mouse. The point is, I asked you not to think about Donald Duck and you did. The chances are you did. Now why did you do that? Are you a particularly awkward person? Are you someone who always does what you're asked not to do? Or are you just a normal person like everyone else who, when they're told not to do something, has to think about what it is they're not going to do before they don't do it? Similarly, if you think about what you don't want, then that is at the forefront of your mind and interferes with you concentrating on what you do want.

Look back at your list of goals and check whether any are set in the negative. If so, change them into positives. So instead of 'I don't want to be in debt any more', 'I want to have enough money – more than enough money – to pay my bills.' Instead of 'I don't want to be working for anybody else', try 'I want to run my own business.' Notice how you can change things: it makes such a difference. You can also turn them into affirmations to repeat regularly through the day, though you don't have to believe them at first:

I am always able to pay my bills.
I run my own, successful business.

Ten steps to goal setting

Step 1   What do you really, really want?

Have you decided on whatever it is you really, really want? Stop focusing on what you don't want and start concentrating on what you do want. If your first thoughts are about what you don't want, consider how you would prefer things to be. Knowing what you don't want is a great source of information. Perhaps you can ask yourself why you don't want whatever it is and start to think about the alternatives. What do you want instead?

Sally left her job and left London because she had 'had enough'. She no longer wanted to work in an atmosphere that she felt was stifling her and stunting any thoughts of progress. She had drifted in and out of work and just knew it was time to take stock. She was very clear about what she didn't want from work. She had no other job in mind, just knew she had to get away. Once removed from the 'heat', she was able to switch her attention to the future.

Step 2   Be clear and specific

Are you as clear and specific as you can be? Replace 'be less stressed' with 'I will take five minutes a day on my own', or 'When I get in from work I will sit and read the paper/listen to music, etc., before I do anything else.'

Sally wanted to feel valued in the work that she did and decided to look for a job that offered her a clear review procedure. She wanted to be measured and to be able to track her progress. It also was clear to Sally that she wanted to work in a place whose values mirrored hers.

Step 3   Take small steps

Do you take one step at a time? Your goal may relate to a time in the distant future – three or more years. That's a long time to wait for success. So . . . break it down into bite-sized pieces. They could be as small as something you can do every day towards your goal, or a weekly, monthly or six-monthly target.

Roy was told he needed to get fit to stay alive. He liked swimming but couldn't imagine going three times a week and swimming for at least 30 minutes. At first he just didn't go. I asked him how long he imagined he could manage. A flippant 'five minutes' was his answer. So that's what he started with. After the first five minutes, he managed another five minutes, then another and then another. He now does at least eighteen lots of five minutes' swimming a week.

Step 4   Whose goals?

Are you sure that your goals are *your* goals? They need to fit in with what's important for you. If you are making a change in your life to suit someone else, it may not fit in with your beliefs and values. If the word 'should' or 'ought' is in your goal, just check who says so. Unless you live in splendid isolation you will want to feel comfortable with the end result. Such thoughts may lead you to refine or rethink aspects of your final objective. So consider any impact your goals could have on the people around you.

Step 5   Record them

Have you written down your goals and put them somewhere you can see them? Collect articles from papers and magazines that remind you of where you are going. If you stick pigs on your fridge door because you want to lose weight, understand that you are creating a negative picture. It may help to remind you what you want to get away from. It may also stop you creating a positive picture of how you want to be. Find items that represent your goals in a positive way.

Throw away your fat pig fridge magnets. The intention may be to act as a warning and frightening reminder of what might be or has been. The effect is to reinforce the image. What other cues are there around your house, car or office creating the images you want to leave behind? Replace them with more constructive, positive ones.

Step 6   What are you saying?

Check: what are you saying to yourself about yourself regarding your goals? Notice any negatives like 'I'll never be able to do that. I can't. That's not the sort of thing I do.' If you say and believe statements like these about yourself, you won't allow yourself to change. Words like 'This is something I can do, I won't know until I've had a go' are much more helpful.

I often ask people if they are limited by the 'terrible toos'. 'Too old', 'too young', 'too fat', 'too thin', 'too tired'... What's yours? The chances are they're an indication that what you've targeted isn't exactly what you want. If you're too tired to take on your goal, what do you have enough energy for? If you're too old, who says there is an age limit? It's well worth checking whether or not you are using excuses to get you out of something which makes you uncomfortable, or whether there is another deeper fear stopping you from taking the potential risk.

Step 7   In whose hands?

Are you sure that your goal depends on you for its fulfilment? If you need someone else to change in order to achieve your goal, you lose your control and risk becoming a passive spectator in your own life.

Sally would have stayed in her job if she had been able to get her manager to give her the regular meetings and feedback she requested. For a long time she waited for her boss to make the desired changes and then she realized that nothing was going to happen. The only person whose behaviour she could definitely modify was her own. She was happy to know she was in charge of her own destiny and a little scared, once she resigned, that she couldn't hide behind anyone else's ineptitude.

Step 8   How do you know?

How will you know when you have achieved your goals? Think about how you can measure, especially for the bite-sized pieces. It may be obvious, but if you can't measure them how will you know when you have got where you want to be?

When my goal is to write a book I start by breaking it down into chapter headings, and then further down into the issues to be covered in each chapter. I can tick off each segment as I write it and know that I am on the way towards completion. I also use different colours to signify which draft stage I am in. Purple means it's ready to go to the publishers. Hooray!

Step 9   Practise

Rehearse in your mind and imagine yourself having achieved what you want. Use your imagination fully. Take some time to sit or lie down quietly and concentrate on being where you want to be. Picture yourself, hear yourself and give yourself a sense of what it feels like when you are there.

Suki was able to imagine herself in the house she wanted. She could see the brightly painted living room with all her familiar bits and pieces. She could hear her children laughing and shouting as they investigated all the rooms. She felt excited and comfortable settling into her new surroundings. She started to smell fresh-baked bread and then stopped before it turned into burnt toast.

Step 10   Rewards

Do you find ways to encourage and reward yourself as you achieve? Celebrate all successes, however small, and forgive any relapses. It is important to acknowledge that the dreary bits are all part of the whole goal. If you have plodded through some tedious actions, celebrate because they are going to take you where you want to be.

Rewards can vary from time to yourself or ringing a good friend to going out, buying yourself a gift, reading a magazine from cover to cover, doing something you've promised yourself for ages and haven't got around to yet or collecting tokens along the way to cash in when you decide to. Organize a 'success log' that you can look at and remind yourself how far you've got. Check whether you need to review and modify. If you find yourself giving up then maybe it's not your goal.

Roy became so keen on swimming and the buzz he got from exercise that he decided he wanted to make it a greater part of his life. He was never going to be a gold medal athlete but he was able to help others enjoy getting fit and healthy. He pestered the staff in his local gym, and was taken on as a receptionist with a view to studying and becoming a trainee fitness instructor.

Don't be afraid if your goals change. As you start to carry out the actions you might find yourself changing direction on the way. Be flexible and you will find opportunities that you didn't even know existed before you started on your journey.

I know someone who was convinced they wanted to be an academic in their chosen subject of geology. They got as far as starting their PhD before realizing that they wanted to spend their life in Lanzarote, which they had visited on many field trips. They had thought that the geology study was the key until they returned to Lanzarote for a holiday and knew that was where they wanted to be. They stopped the PhD, learnt Spanish and set up a centre for geologists to stay and study in. They became so much a part of the community that they branched out into general tourism and set up a successful holiday location.

Think about:

- How would you be if you could have what you want?
- How will you know when you've got it?
- If you were to achieve your goal, how would you feel?
- How does it fit in with other parts of your life?

Since I started researching, reading and writing this book, I have become absorbed again in the ideas and processes for myself. In terms of goal setting and dreaming about the future there is a specific question that I keep encountering, namely, where are the gaps? It seems so obvious and yet it's not often asked this way.

Question

What are the gaps that prevent you from achieving your goals?

There may be a number of reasons or barriers stopping you from getting what you want, and many of them will be uncovered in the following chapters. You could discover that you are missing something in the area of time, organization, sense of self, control, companionship, energy, wealth or well-being. They may have already shown up in the first exercise. In the table below, list anything that is missing for you and then start to think about some small actions you can take to set the wheels in action. Like Roy, who started swimming in five-minute intervals, what one thing might you do now to know you are doing something towards your goal?

What's missing?	What can I start doing?

If you don't make decisions about how you are going to live in years to come, then you have already made a decision – to be directed by the environment instead of shaping your own destiny.

(Robbins, 1992)

Shift 2
Who says you should?

We hold all kinds of ideas and perceptions in our minds about the way the world is and the way it should be. Each of us has our own unique experience of life and our responses to similar situations can be quite different. It is important to understand what has shaped the significant aspects of our personality. Once we have that comprehension then we have the potential to change.

In most cultures and families there are written and unwritten rules about what is acceptable or unacceptable behaviour. As a small child you would have absorbed a lot of information from the people around you. They told you how you should behave, what kind of person to be, what to expect from the world and how others should behave towards you. These internalized rules would be given as either permissions or injunctions.

Permissions are positive and developmental, they encourage a child to experiment and learn about themselves in an accepting atmosphere. They may include such statements as: 'It's fine to ask for help', 'You can learn from your mistakes', 'You're gorgeous because you're you', 'No matter what anyone says you'll always be a worthwhile person.'

Injunctions are negative and suppress growth. They may include statements like: 'Big boys don't cry', 'Why can't you be like . . .', 'You've no idea how to . . .', 'Beauty is only skin deep', 'I want doesn't get.'

You may find that you remember permissions or injunctions relating to specific areas of your life. Were you given messages about expressing feelings, being emotionally close, being who you are, being your age, making mistakes, or being successful?

In the main, all these messages are given with an underlying love and care, though they are not always received that way. Sometimes they are the result of tension in the giver and more of a throwaway statement, like, 'Leave me alone' or 'I'm too exhausted to think this through', which a young child can internalize as a personal rule. In this case, they may become withdrawn or quiet. I often suggest that clients consider whether their parents (or they as parents) wake up in the morning and consciously think what messages they can give out to ensure that their children are neurotic, unhinged and lead miserable lives. Though that might be the outcome, I am sure that it is not the intention. Very often they are simply repeating the messages and rules that they were given, not realizing that they were questionable. I believe that we all treat others in the best way we can with the knowledge and understanding we have at the time. It is easy to look back and criticize the messages we've received, but not very constructive. As we grow up we assume that the way our family operates is the way all families operate. Any differences are deviant on someone else's part, not ours.

How often have you heard of a person in a position of power recounting to their child or subordinate, 'No-one helped me, I learned the hard way. It didn't do me any harm and it won't do you any'? There is no doubt that at some level the speaker believes that they are helping the other person build character and self-reliance. At another level they probably have no strategy for reaching out with compassion.

As children we often develop behaviours to fit whichever rules we've given most attention. As they are more or less successful, so the behaviour becomes automatic and habitual. As adults we are often unaware of why we do things the way we do and are relieved when we find different ways of living. Once you have found the source of your behaviour, you can increase your choice to change.

Jaz knew that he would eventually follow his parents into the business they had inherited from his grandparents just after he was born. He was encouraged to study at college after finishing school, and it was agreed that a law degree would hold him in good stead. Jaz was a bright and able student who managed to get through his studies without being passionately involved in them. He was most popular at college for the cartoons and caricatures he drew of fellow students and the teaching staff. Once he graduated, Jaz started to work his way through the business and eventually took over as MD when his father retired. Things moved along steadily and he introduced his own ideas to make the business more attractive and successful. Unfortunately a serious stock-market crash meant that creditors were unable to pay up and the business was declared bankrupt. A moment of choice for Jaz. He fell into a depression and remembered as a child hearing, 'You never stick at things.' Eventually his friends encouraged him to get out and do something, anything. He says he doesn't know why, but he went to evening classes and studied art. Within three months he realized that this was what he had always wanted to do. At the age of 55 he had found his vocation.

He resisted any temptation to waste time regretting that he hadn't done it before. Instead, he enjoyed the thrill of finding out what he wanted to do, doing it and being valued and recognized in the art world.

We have some very strong messages relating to the worlds of work and study. In some families there is no question that further education is a given, not a choice. In others, emphasis is placed on the first pay packet as soon as school is over. Neither of these is right or wrong, and both can be beneficial or limiting. I remember the horror at school when one of the girls decided to leave straight after her exams and start work as a model. This was not what she was educated for. I, too, was shocked and also secretly admiring of such rebellion. I now know that it would have been great if we could have been set the task of assessing which of her transferable skills and learnings she might take from school into her modelling career. (Though I guess that is a bit of a radical notion.)

Question

What were the rules in your family?

Some people feel as if their whole lives have been mapped out for them before they even get to school because of the future roles that have been 'decided' for them. 'We've always had plumbers in our family, it's a good steady job. People always need plumbers.' 'Of course you'll be a teacher, that's what the girls in this family do. You can always go back to it after you've had your children.' How loaded these seemingly simple statements are, and how full of assumptions.

Family sayings

From a very early age the die may be cast and a career or life path is embarked upon without question. That's fine when the family choice is also the individual's choice, but not so good when it doesn't fit. Some of us just sigh and get on with it, while others resist and drop out somehow. The pressure is often conveyed through family sayings, such as, 'Think of the poor starving children . . .', 'I want never gets . . .', 'Pride comes before a fall . . .', 'Don't get too big for your boots . . .'. Once again when we go to school, we are given new permissions and injunctions about the way we should behave. Without realizing or questioning we take these 'rules' on board, and they can become part of our automatic guidelines for living. Sometimes they only need to be stated once at a very impressionable time or by a very significant person and they become unquestionably part of our lives.

Molly was told as a young girl many years ago that if she touched a man's penis before she was married she would contract a sexually transmitted disease (std) and infect any children she had. Molly's one incident happened when she was fifteen and got carried away one night with her boyfriend. She immediately ended the relationship and never went out with anyone else. In her late fifties Molly went to the doctor for a blood test and asked if they could check for std too. She was horrified when she knew the truth and realized how much she had missed in her life.

The saddest part is that Molly's mother was probably trying to protect her and make sure she wasn't sexually active and didn't get pregnant before she was married (something which mattered to Molly's mother, and her generation, possibly more than it mattered to Molly). She couldn't possibly have realized the effect she would have on her impressionable daughter's life.

Take a moment to write or tape-record any injunctions and negative messages you remember receiving from any significant people and authority figures. These could include your parents, siblings, other family members, peers, teachers, youth leaders, religious figures, bosses, workmates and neighbours. (What will the neighbours think?) Once you have them in front of you or where you can hear them, write or shout the response: *'Lies, lies, lies!'* Then decide what messages you would prefer instead and make them into affirmations, new beliefs you can repeat regularly.

One of my first jobs was as a research assistant in a university. Part of the work involved writing draft papers for my professor to amend and publish. She often told me (it may only have been once, but I remember it as 'always') 'This is no good, you can't write.' I was young, impressionable and insecure enough at that point in my life to believe her. Even after leaving that job I struggled to put pen to paper when creating workbooks and handouts for training purposes. When I was invited to submit a chapter for my first book I nearly refused before the first fence. Happily I was cajoled and supported and am now a nearly prolific writer. When I wrote (!) my list of negative messages, one was 'I can't write.' My preferred message now is: 'I can write well about non-academic, personal development issues. They interest me and I am passionate about them.' In one sense my boss had been correct, but I never sought the clarification that I wrote inappropriately for the academic world, to which I was not suited.

Permissions

We need to balance up this section by listing at least five permissions leading to positive qualities that you inherited from the important people around you. It may be that your parents or guardians were always encouraging you, or that a particular teacher believed in you and gave you confidence. It can be very easy to overlook or forget these when we are in our 'no good' moods.

I remember the following that serve me well:

'We'll always love you' – quality: lovable
'You are a fun-loving person who's good to be with' – quality: humour
'You take time to care for others' – quality: compassion
'You speak your mind' – quality: honesty
'We are a close family' – quality: sense of belonging

The tyranny of shoulds

Another way of recognizing messages that have been handed down and may no longer be (if they ever were) facilitative is to notice statements that contain the words 'should', 'ought' or 'must'. If we try to motivate or run our lives through the 'should' statements we received we can feel pressured and resentful. It's as if some outside force is ruling us from within and we have no control. It's like having a parrot sitting on our shoulder constantly repeating someone else's orders. (These are the statements affirmations can overrule.) Sadly, we tend to end up feeling lethargic, unmotivated and weighed down. This is often accompanied by an end result of feeling guilty. When we expect others to conform to our 'should' statements we usually end up annoyed and frustrated. When they fall short of our rigid expectations, as is sometimes inevitable, we feel bitter and self-righteous. Just think of the time and energy we waste worrying about it, too.

The way we choose to live our lives is often shaped by these 'laws', and it never occurs to us that we have the power to change them. The first step towards changing them is to notice their existence. Next time you come across a statement starting with 'I should' or 'I ought' or 'I must', ask yourself 'Why?' and 'What will happen if I don't?' (with 'shouldn't', 'oughtn't' or 'mustn't', then the second question is 'What will happen if I do?'). Immediately you start to question these notions you create the element of choice. What may have been useful in your past could become limiting now.

Hamish was determined to lose weight and was doing well. His main concern was around eating out, which was something he did with his work as well as socially. The servings were bigger than he wanted but he couldn't bring himself to leave any. Not surprising when you look at his 'shoulds' around food.

Compare:

I must:	eat everything on my plate.
Why?	It is rude, ungrateful, churlish to leave any. There are children starving in Africa.
If I don't?	People will think me rude and reject me. It's my fault there isn't enough food to go round.

With:

I could:	eat everything on my plate.
Choice:	And I have the choice.
If I don't?	People will recognize that I know when to stop. I am learning to assess how much I want. There are more constructive ways I can help the starving in Africa.

Are there any of your 'shoulds' that might benefit from a similar analysis? This is something you can do with a friend. Using the table on the next page, challenge each other to assess what happens when you exercise your choice. You can also substitute the question 'Why haven't I?' for 'If I don't' and see what kind of answers you come up with. Sometimes this taps into old concepts that you have about yourself of being mean, lazy, etc., that you no longer need or want to hold on to.

As a first step, then, notice which 'rules' run your life. Accept them, don't judge them, and consider how you might start to change them. You may find it helps to work out what the positive intention was behind the rules; that way you're more likely to feel OK about

I should/ought/must: ———————————————

Why? ——————————————————

If I don't? ————————————————
I could ——————————————————

Choice: And I have the choice

If I don't? ——————————————————

   or

Why haven't I? ——————————————————

them and the person who gave them to you. You might even decide to create replacement rules that better fit your values. Of course, some of the 'shoulds' will fit well into your philosophy and you can happily keep them around you in the form of 'I could . . . and I choose to . . .'

Another 'anti-should' device is to have a checklist of the advantages and disadvantages of the 'required behaviour', as the table opposite.

Try this exercise a few times and you may find yourself changing the way you want to behave. Understand your motives and how you've arrived at them. Then let yourself start to meet your needs differently. See Shift 6, 'Behave yourself', for ideas on how to put the changed messages into action.

Beliefs

Beliefs represent the assumptions we make about ourselves, others in the world and how we expect things to be. These assumptions determine the way we behave and shape our decision-making processes. They are often based on emotions rather than facts. We tend to notice 'facts' that reinforce the beliefs. For example, if you believe that 'everyone is easy to get along with', you will only notice how well you interact with people. If, however, your belief is that 'you can't trust anyone', you will be suspicious and expect to be duped. The chances are you will give that impression, too, and people will be wary of you. Hence the term 'self-fulfilling prophecy' – what you believe about yourself is what happens to you. Beliefs develop from the rules and messages we receive as children.

I must please others, then they will accept and appreciate me

Advantages	Disadvantages
I will keep my job because my boss knows I will always finish her work however long it takes	Exhaustion and stress
	Whenever others are unhappy I'll feel guilty and assume it's my fault
My family know they don't have to worry or think about their needs and will be happy	
	I'll end up blaming them and feeling resentful because I always come last and am not meeting my needs
The school knows I'll be there for any fundraising events and will always bake or sew for them	
	I won't like myself when I back down in arguments over which I have strong feelings
	There may be peace outside but inside there will be a war waging in which I'll be adding to my misery by being angry with myself for being such a doormat

Annemarie had grown up in rural France with the belief that you have to work hard to get what you want from life. Over many years she built up a small business consisting of a shop which sold fashionable and expensive artefacts for tourists to her region. She spent every weekday in the shop and then bought her stock at the weekends. She couldn't afford any help and didn't dare leave the shop unattended during opening hours in case she lost custom. She felt she was on a treadmill, but also believed that she must continue to work hard so that one day she could afford to stop and live the life she wanted. She was waiting for all her hard work to be rewarded.

The trouble is that she was stuck into believing she had to keep working until magically she would be relieved. Of course, it doesn't work that way even though many of us are in the bind of believing that it does.

17

Annemarie was rescued by a friend who took a completely different perspective. Had she ever thought about moving back to her lovely house in the rural countryside and opening it up for American tourists? She could take them round the France she knows and loves, translate for them and take them to all the 'off the beaten track' places they liked to visit. So instead of working hard she could play more and enjoy a social life in a way she had not experienced for many years. This was a scary and exciting idea for Annemarie. She took up the challenge and was soon conscious of the opportunities that were available to her.

Have you ever encountered someone who keeps telling you that no-one can help them? No matter what you do or say they always have a reason why it's not right for them. In the end you probably give up – and so successfully reinforce their belief that no-one can help them. They are not being deliberately obstructive, even though it may seem that way. They have held that belief for many years and would have to face many challenges in order to let it go. These beliefs are so familiar that we often don't know they are there until someone starts to ask questions like: 'Who says so?', 'What would happen if someone could help you?'

Begin to notice which beliefs drive your thoughts, feelings and actions. If your beliefs are restrictive and limiting, discard them. If they are supportive and empowering, keep them and live by them.

Moment of choice

How do you choose what to believe? It may well be the case that you have beliefs that you no longer need; their purpose is obsolete. If that is so, then change them. You can choose whatever you want to believe. Sometimes we choose, or have imposed on us, beliefs that are restrictive in nature. We bring them with us into all kinds of situations. Once we recognize them, we can choose to replace them or discard them completely. If you approach the question from the other side you may be following the belief 'I have learnt many things in my life, now is the time to update my repertoire.'

Whether you believe 'I can change' or whether you believe 'I can't change', the chances are you will be proven right until you investigate the origin of the belief further. Your beliefs can either work with you and for you or despite you and against you. Look at the table below.

I can change	I can't change
'I enjoy new ideas' 'I know I can change' 'I've learnt so much before, here's another opportunity' 'I've an open mind'	'You can't teach an old dog new tricks' 'I never pick up new ideas' 'They said I was stupid at school . . .' 'I've tried things like this before – they never work' 'Nothing will make me change'

Question

What's stopping you change?

Some of the most common answers I receive to that question are:

- waiting for the right time;
- waiting until I have time;
- waiting for someone to notice (I'm sad, unhappy, overworked, under-resourced, tired, needing something);
- waiting for a knight on a white charger to whisk me away from all this;
- waiting for someone else to make the first move;
- waiting for someone to say they're sorry;
- waiting until I have worked hard enough to stop;
- waiting until I've paid off all my bills.

As you add any others that you're specifically waiting for, check whether they relate to any belief that is pushing you that way. Then think how you can start to make some changes that will facilitate your life.

What would happen if you stopped waiting and started acting? It seems to me that it is unlikely to be any worse than the limbo of waiting that you're in at the moment. Once you are moving in some direction you will find your motivation has changed and you are ready to take control of your life. How freeing! If you think back to Shift 1, with all your goals and dreams, you may well find that you are now more aware of what's held you back from starting on them. Take some time out to review your limiting beliefs and consider how to make them empowering for you.

Question

Which of your beliefs helps or hinders you?

If you hold the belief 'I must not make mistakes' and you want to change it, here's a way to do so:

Q 1 Is this an empowering belief? To which you might answer 'no'. It is the kind of belief that stops some people from trying out something new.

Q 2 Is this a limiting belief? A 'yes' answer is likely here.

Q 3 Where has it come from? The answer here could be school, parents or any authority figures. I ask this question so you can clarify whose belief it is.

Q 4 What was the positive intention behind it? This takes away any sense of blaming and enables understanding of why you were given it. The answer then may focus around wanting to encourage you to do your best, something you might not have understood at the time.

Q 5 How do you want to change it? Here you can substitute a new empowering belief to start telling yourself instead: 'I can make mistakes and I can learn from them.' Create a belief that is yours and is relevant to you.

Fill in the table below and decide whether or not you want to change your beliefs.

Belief	Empowering	Restricting	Source	Intention	Change
I must not make mistakes	No	Yes	School	Best performance	I can learn from my mistakes

Shift 3
Time for a clear out

Many of us are quite used to the notion of spring-cleaning. The winter is gone and it's time to spring towards the summer and sunny months. It's a bit like emerging from hibernation or a chrysalis, and we often feel inspired towards a fresh and clean start. This shift gives you the opportunity and some techniques to do the same thing for your mind. Many people I know take time in December to review their year, clear out the debris and plan for the next one. Of course, none of us has to wait until any particular day, month or season before being able to start the process.

> Clutter accumulates when energy stagnates and vice versa . . . The more of it you have, the more stagnant energy it attracts to itself.
>
> (Kingston, 1998)

Clutter begins as a symptom of what is going on in our lives and then adds to the problem itself. So it's a good idea to have a clear out and reassess what matters to you and what doesn't. Decide what you are hanging on to that is outdated and no longer part of your image. It can be surprising how much our ideas and needs change over the years. Get into the habit of assessment and review on a regular basis. Start now and design a routine to enable you to systematically shed the things from your life that bog you down and to develop and consolidate the patterns that can take you to where you want to be. You've already set some goals and decided on some actions in Shift 1; now you can create the space in your life to embrace them. There are many areas in which we can apply the spring-clean analogy. I would like to encourage you to consider the following: your mind, your space and your emotions.

Imagine

Imagine being able to go inside your head with a brightly coloured feather duster and waft away the debris and cobwebs that have accumulated in your life up to now.

Start by concentrating on your breathing and allow yourself to relax into your chair or on the floor if you are lying down.

Enjoy the thought that you are going to release any tension and know that you deserve the time you are giving yourself.

Relax and breathe slowly.

Focus on your mind. How much 'rubbish' is in there and how many dustbin bags or packing boxes might you fill once you start to remove it? As you dust, polish and sort, allow yourself a split second to decide whether there is anything worth keeping from each of these relics before you discard them.

They all happened for a reason, and your challenge is to accept the learning and understanding while letting go of the negative emotions that surround them.

Then decide what kind of receptacle all the unwanted items, ideas, thoughts or beliefs are going into and start to fill it. Notice how you feel as you wander through your past. Are you light, heavy, floating or dragged down? If you want to, you can climb or jump into the container and stamp around or float through the collection.

Blow away the redundant items and enjoy the clear space that you are creating, ready to welcome in anything new that you desire.

When you have sorted all you want, start to leave your mind and move back to the room you are in. Be ready to open your eyes, feeling great and inspired, free of some of your unhelpful clutter.

Make this a daydream you can rerun any time you want to shift your clutter.

No time?

In the world of work and management, masses of time and money is spent on sending people on courses to better manage their time. The irony is that they will often say they don't have time to put the theories and exercises into practice. Sound familiar? We are sometimes so preoccupied with worries and problems that we honestly believe we don't have any more time to consider sorting or letting them go. I've even had clients tell me that they become worried if it appears that they don't have anything to worry about. Sounds daft, but it happens, and without realizing it they are filling their minds with lots of unhelpful clutter. The key question I often ask is: 'What do you have time for?' which can be a good indicator of where their priorities lie. In many cases, it isn't time we're short of, but direction. Direction creates time and motivation creates energy. We certainly have plenty of energy for the things we want to do. Perhaps it would be better if we changed the emphasis and talked about managing ourselves rather than our time.

Question

How much information can you hold?

There is a theory that the conscious brain can only hold on to a maximum of nine pieces of information at any one time. These can be internal thoughts and feelings or external events and activities. Obviously there are many things that we do on a daily basis without having to think consciously about them. You weren't aware of the task of reading these words until I just wrote about it, and you probably weren't thinking about the texture of the book or the sounds going on around you until I raised your awareness. And so it should be. If we used all our conscious energy thinking about things we do 'naturally' and automatically, then we wouldn't have space to do anything else. It is no wonder, though, that sometimes we complain of 'information overload', when our brains feel as if they cannot take in any new information or ideas, otherwise we'll burst. It also explains why you have an idea one minute and lose it the next because something or someone has interrupted your thinking.

When we're really overloaded the only time the thoughts can re-emerge is during the early hours of the morning, when there is nothing to obstruct them. It makes sense to record your ideas whenever they occur so you know they're available and they're not taking up the space of thoughts that are a priority now. Keep a notebook or tape recorder in a designated place to capture your thoughts and ideas. This way you're not investing any time trying to find them practically or mentally.

If you think about the way you have stored your memories from your past, you may find that those which refer to less happy moments or leave you feeling badly about yourself are closer to the surface than any 'feel good' moments that you have. If this is the case, then the former are likely to slip into consciousness more easily than those hidden a bit further away. They will take up part of your nine pieces of information space. Many of us hold on to insults, name-calling and criticisms for many years while releasing compliments and praise often without even acknowledging them. The insults get 'stuck' in our conscious brain and seriously hinder our chances of success in whatever way we desire it. As soon as you notice them entering your consciousness, release them and make space to collect the plaudits and good things that come your way.

'That happened in the past. My mind is now positively focused.'

When I started working as a management trainer I was involved in a series of four-day residential courses in communication skills. At the end of each course I would sit with my colleagues on the train journey home, with a stiff drink and the evaluation forms. In the main they were excellent and a joy to read, but invariably there would be one or two negative comments and I would use these to beat myself up and remind myself that I wasn't that good really. How sad that I would discount the delegates who appreciated and benefited from the training and completely accept the criticisms, or focus on them and become highly defensive. And what a waste of conscious energy to put myself down that way. As I have become more experienced and confident I am better able to celebrate the good news and rationally respond to the criticisms.

This, then, is a very important area for clearing out. Whatever has happened or been said to you before now, is done, it's over. You can't change it, though you can alter its effect or its hold on you. You can now decide how much of it is going to take up space in your conscious mind. While you're worrying about what you said or did yesterday or yesteryear, you are using up valuable conscious brain space that could be focusing on whatever you want now and for the rest of your life.

Whatever confronts us today, some day will be just a memory ... Today's newspaper crisis is tomorrow's fish and chip wrapping.

(Roet, 2000)

Don't worry

Find a pigeon-hole deep in the recesses of your mind where you can file away your worries. Worrying is one of the mind's biggest time robbers. As you worry about the past or the future you are wasting valuable energy which you could use much more productively. Worrying creates so much clutter in your mind that you cannot think clearly about anything. When you do find yourself worrying, consider an alternative way of thinking about the situation and change the thought. Redress the balance by remembering what has worked in your life around the worrying issue, or accept that it is happening and that worrying won't change it. What can you do? If there is anything you can do, work out what and how, and do it. If nothing, think what you might do differently next time and how you are going to move on. Take on the Buddhist mantra: 'Just for today, I will not worry or get angry.' Insert any emotion that fits.

Letting go

> Resentments bind you to the past with chains of steel and block up your readiness to receive future benefits.
>
> (Black, 1992)

How would you feel if you didn't hold on to your anger, envy, shame or any other unhelpful emotions? What would you be missing? I ask that question because sometimes it seems as though these emotions are so much a part of you that you can't imagine yourself without them. People wouldn't recognize you or know who you were without the usual put-downs aimed at them or yourself. They know what to expect from you now, and might even challenge you without your prejudices and value judgements. In a strange way it is often the reaction of people around us that can prevent us from changing.

> Ryan was always late meeting with his friends. He decided that he had had enough of the upset he caused them and the stress he sometimes put himself under. He started planning so that he could be more punctual more often. Of course, this threw his friends completely, and instead of welcoming and congratulating him for his timekeeping, they teased him unmercifully. 'You're on time, did you think we were meeting yesterday?' Ryan felt so dispirited by their reactions that he decided it wasn't worth the aggravation to be on time and easily slipped back into his old ways. He didn't want to, but felt too uncomfortable not to. The only time he was able to practise being on time was with new friends and acquaintances who didn't have any 'late' expectations.

Imagine the space and freedom you could create for yourself to have a positive and enjoyable approach to life if you decided to let go of your negative emotions. Only you can make it happen. You have to believe that you deserve a fulfilled and rewarding life. A new you might take some getting used to and can be scary at first, even if it's the you you genuinely desire. Each time you notice a new response or different behaviours, be pleased, congratulate yourself and build up a rewards bank or go for instant prizes, whichever works better for you. You might want to reward yourself with time, five minutes for every risk taken which can build up to many minutes or hours for yourself to cash in when you want, as long as you cash them in regularly. You could take a walk, relax to soothing music, read a book, have a bath. The list is endless and for you to extend. If you close yourself off to the opportunities around you, they'll wander by without you even noticing them. Be open and ready to receive the surprises you'll encounter on your travels. Spend more time with people who support and encourage you.

Forgive to release

One of the hardest and yet most satisfying things you can do is to start forgiving yourself and other people. Anything that has happened in the past belongs there, and you can do nothing about it. While you don't forgive, you are holding on to some of the most time-consuming and destructive clutter around you. What's the point of using up your maximum of nine pieces of conscious information with something you can't influence in any way?

My key learning about forgiveness, and one that moved me forward hugely in my life, was when I understood that by forgiving I am not condoning bad or unacceptable behaviour, but I am releasing the negative energy that surrounds it. I used to think forgiveness was tantamount to approval, saying, 'OK, fine. You hurt me badly but it doesn't matter, just carry on . . .'; I now understand that when I forgive I move on. When I don't I am rooted to the same spot or even move backwards in my own despair. It's my choice and my emotional health that is affected.

If I stay hurt, depressed, angry, frustrated or humiliated (to name but a few options) I affect me much more than anyone else. Others may notice that I'm antisocial or crabby from time to time, but the bad feelings are with me all the time. Have you ever fumed at someone for years and then decided to 'have it out' with them, only to find that they haven't a clue what you're talking about? They've completely forgotten the incident or remembered it very differently, and you hung on to it, almost caressing it occasionally, just to remember how badly they treated you. You are the one who's been consumed by it, and they've released it long ago. When you come to reflect on it, it's often not that big a deal.

When it is a big deal and someone has hurt you immensely, then it is even more important to forgive them so that their impact on you is diluted as soon as possible. You owe it to yourself to survive and grow despite them rather than remain stuck because of them. They have damaged you once: don't give them the power to keep you down for ever. When we withhold forgiveness, *we* suffer. Blaming others or ourselves gets us nowhere. What is done is done, and can't be undone. We can choose to learn from it and decide to prevent it happening again.

Fran told me about the horrible time she had at her son's wedding. Her ex-husband was there with his new, young wife. He seemed to be flaunting his new wife and generally misbehaving. Fran was sure 'he only behaved that way to get at me'. My guess is that she was the last thing on his mind and he was probably wanting approval rather than anything else.

Moment of choice

It's easier to act your way into a new way of thinking than to think your way into a new way of acting.

(Millard Fuller, founder and president of
Habitat for Humanity International)

You can choose to live the life you want or you can choose to live the life others might try to give you. Remember the affirmation: 'Whatever you say or do to me, I am still a worthwile person.' Believe and repeat it regularly. Then you will be much more in charge of your life. Forgiveness will help you to let go of any unhealthy relationships and make you available for healthier, more nurturing ones.

I have worked with many people who have found themselves rejected, redundant or, in some way, surplus to requirements. At the time they often feel devastated, useless and furious that they could be so poorly treated. Their choice of how to consider responding to the situation can lead to different outcomes. For some it becomes the turning point that enables them to take risks and achieve far more than they would have previously. It frees them up to realize that nothing is forever or guaranteed, so they can start living in the present and embrace new challenges.

Others are stuck in 'it shouldn't have happened to me' and 'it's not fair, what did I do to deserve this?' grooves. They are loading themselves up with unhelpful clutter which will keep them in a victim position and can leave them helpless. It's almost as though they have to stay in a bad emotional and physical place to prove to the world how badly they have been treated. Sadly, either the world will grow tired of them and leave them alone or people around them can be dragged down with them in a negative spiral.

> Two men looked out through the prison bars. One saw mud, the other the stars.
>
> (Dale Carnegie)

Which way do you look when things go against you? When you focus on the mud, you can get stuck and bogged down; when you look up to the stars you feel hope and energy.

Question

What would happen if you let go of your feelings of anger, hurt or resentment and forgave their source?

If it involves someone other than yourself, they don't need to know about your forgiving them: this is for you. The chances are that they don't have any idea how much energy you are expending holding on to the feelings anyway. Whatever happened to you won't unhappen, but you will have increased mental space to create a new and compelling future for yourself, without bringing them along. It was bad enough for you at the time and it doesn't have to dominate or run your life for ever.

There are many ways you can forgive and let go of the debilitating emotions. Think about what would work best for you. Some people find that writing it down and reliving the experience releases the strong emotions and shows them that they have survived and are moving on. That is why there are so many books about kidnap, rape and abusive relationships. By telling their story the authors want to eliminate their demons and help others recognize that there is a way forward.

You could:

- Write a letter to whomever you want to forgive. Don't send it, but destroy it and let it go. Or tape what you want to say, then erase it and release the feelings.
- Record your story and try to understand what was happening for you and them. Then create an affirmation that allows you to start the rest of your life now.

I forgive everyone, I forgive myself. I forgive all past experience.
Forgiving everyone, forgiving myself. I am free. I am free.

(Hay, 1988)

Imagine

Use your imagination to lessen the impact of past hurts and enable
their release. The exercise below starts with a memory of the
incident and enables you to change its influence on your mind. This
is a common technique that diminishes the incident and the feelings
by substituting more acceptable ones. If you repeat the exercise you
will find that the memory changes and takes less room in your mind
than before.

Think briefly how you would like to replace it.

Start by concentrating on your breathing and allow yourself to
relax into your chair or on the floor if you are lying down.

Enjoy the thought that you are going to release any tension
and know that you deserve the time you are giving yourself.

Relax and breathe slowly.

Remember the scene(s) in your mind and gradually reduce
their size. Change the colour to make them grey and
unattractive. If there are any sounds attached, mute them.
Notice any uncomfortable sensations or feelings and tell
yourself to cancel them because you want to change them.
None of them serves you any longer.

Then start to replace them with the scenes you want from
now on. Elaborate the new pictures with rousing and motivating music. Experience joyous feelings and sensations. Enjoy
the present and future that you want.

Remember that you have complete control over your
imagination here. Experiment with colours, sounds and sensations. Any that don't work, remove. Any that do work, make
them bigger, brighter, louder and bolder.

Return to the present and notice what happens and how you
feel when you recall the memory; its effect on you will have
changed and its power will have diminished or disappeared
completely.

TIME FOR A CLEAR OUT

As you clear out your emotional clutter, you will create plenty of space for new, positive emotions. You will also be making space for new and enriching relationships. Our minds can become as cluttered as our sock drawer, and it's great when we can open them without a struggle.

> My mind is like a parachute. It only functions when it's open.
>
> (Jon Hendricks, American musician and lyricist)

Shift 4

What are you telling yourself?

You are the person who has the most power over your life.

To some of you this is obvious, while to others it may seem complete nonsense because you feel 'ruled' by your parents, your partner, your children, your work or the world in general. The key point here is that others can only *influence* how you think about yourself. It's not so much what they say or do to you that has a positive or negative effect, it's what you say or do to yourself afterwards that creates your feeling good or bad about yourself. It may well be true that if you hear many times how stupid, cruel or dishonest you are, you begin to believe it and act it out. You wouldn't, though, if you had your own contradictory statements for yourself. When you feel frustrated or upset by a person or a situation, you are not reacting to them but to your feelings about them. These are your feelings and not someone else's fault. Once you recognize and understand this completely, you can start to take responsibility for how you feel, and change it.

> No-one can make me feel inferior without my consent.
>
> (Eleanor Roosevelt)

This Shift is about making your mind more flexible. We are cajoled into thinking that we must attend countless exercise classes to get our bodies moving, flexible and supple. But if our minds aren't right, we're making life difficult for ourselves. Once your mind is on your side, it's a lot easier to get fitter and to become the person you want to be. A key part of the process involves noticing what you say to yourself as you go through your life. When you stop talking about what you *can't* do, and focus on what you *can* do, the results are amazing.

Don't take my word for it. Experience yet again what your mind can do for you, using your wonderful imagination.

Imagine

Start by concentrating on your breathing and allow yourself to relax into your chair or on the floor if you are lying down.

Enjoy the thought that you are going to release any tension and know that you deserve the time you are giving yourself.

Relax and breathe slowly.

Imagine you're in a log cabin, high up in the mountains. It's snowy and cold outside, though the sun is shining brightly and the snow is glistening.

Notice what's around you in the cabin. There are comfortable cushions, some covered in silk, some in velvet. There's a table and some chairs, a dresser in the corner and an old-fashioned cooking range.

You are sitting by a roaring log fire. The flames give out lots of warmth, the wood is glowing in the grate. From the nearby stove, you can smell fresh bread being baked.

The kettle is whistling merrily, signalling that it's time to make yourself a drink if you want one. Just for a moment, enjoy the surroundings.

Notice how you feel. What can you see? What can you hear?

Return to the present and recall the sensations that you experienced.

Perhaps you could hear the kettle whistling, perhaps you could see the fire, or know that the snow outside was cold and you were inside, feeling warm.

Perhaps you could smell the bread, that lovely smell of fresh baking bread.

The point is, where was the log cabin? Was it outside? Were you actually in a log cabin? Of course not. The log cabin is in your mind, and you made it. You created it.

And you can create lots of things in your mind.

A lot of the time, what we create is not the lovely log cabin, not the warmth, not the kettle whistling or the smell of fresh baked bread and the cosy cushions. What we create is what we *don't* want, what we're frightened of. The point is that you can change that to give yourself the feelings, the thoughts and the confidence that you want.

It's much more fun to have your mind working with you rather than against you. The good news is that it's easy – as long as you believe it is. For many years there has been widespread recognition that the mind and body are inextricably linked and that the mind has a controlling influence over us. So if your mind is on your side then your body will follow. In fact, there is a school of thinking that suggests your subconscious works towards making you what you think you are. The messages and thoughts from your mind have a significant influence on the way you feel and the actions you take. In addition, what is in your mind affects your health and well-being. What you think is what you get.

Question

How does your mind work for or against you?

This can be demonstrated in relation to the way that you set yourself up to succeed or set yourself up to fail. It is important to realize that even when we appear to be setting ourselves up for failure there is often a hidden and positive intention behind this behaviour.

One of Dev's goals was to lose two stone in weight. He was on a continuous see-saw of dieting and then making up for lost time (and calories.) He started writing a diary to note how he was sabotaging his diet and what his 'reward' for the sabotage might be. What were the 'benefits' from his remaining overweight? 'People notice me and I make a big impression. I don't have to ask anyone out and risk rejection.'

His next task was to consider how he could still enjoy those 'benefits', if he wanted to, once he had lost weight. This was the most challenging part of his change process. Dev realized that he had felt sure he needed his bulk as protection, and as he came close to his target weight he would break his diet and so not have to risk facing the world without it. He would then also be reinforcing his 'I'm no good, I never succeed' messages. He started to tell himself that he was fine whatever his weight or shape and that he could make a big impression through increased confidence and self-belief. He had the same mind inside whatever figure he portrayed externally. Dev also realized that there was a larger issue for him around commitment and relationships, which he started to work on, too.

We are what we think. All that we are arises with our thoughts. With our thoughts we make our world.

(The Buddha)

There will be days when you feel good, see yourself in a positive light and tell yourself it's a good day. Enjoy them, and from now on think of them as the norm rather than the exception. Have you ever told yourself that things are going too well and something is bound to go wrong? Guess what? Your prediction comes true and so reinforces a 'nothing works or goes right for me' message.

Remember though, *it is only a thought and a thought can be changed*. You can replace your negative self-fulfilling prophecy with a positive one that works for you.

I appreciate and notice all the good things that come my way.

If, deep down, you're partly telling yourself you don't believe it, it won't work so well. Persevere and you will start to see changes despite yourself. Just saying, thinking, experiencing, reading or writing positive thoughts and statements makes us stronger, whether we believe them or not. Our unconscious mind is starting to recognize the possibility that things could be different in our lives, and so they begin to change.

A friend of mine was going on a long-haul flight. She asked me to buy her some painkillers as she always had a bad headache when she flew for any length of time. I was not surprised she had headaches as she was telling her subconscious that was what she expected on the journey. I agreed to buy the painkillers as long as she would say some affirmations. She was reticent at first. 'I don't believe that I can feel relaxed as I travel. I don't believe that I am comfortable and able to sleep when I fly.' However, a deal's a deal, and she repeated the affirmations I gave her: 'I am always relaxed when I fly. I enjoy long flights because I am going to see my friends. I sleep easily when I fly.'

She was delighted to report a much better journey. She still asks me to suggest affirmations for unnerving situations and is beginning to create her own, too. As she collects and uses them, her mind is developing the positive life she wants.

Moment of choice

As you become more aware of your thoughts and how they affect you, you can choose to hold on to the negative ones and be miserable, or change them for ones that are more positive and enabling. The first thing is to notice and think about what you are saying to yourself, what you hear, what you see or how you feel. Awareness means you are conscious of the choices available.

It's better to light the candle than curse the darkness.

(Chinese proverb)

When I was working as a college counsellor I had to go and see the principal about one of my student clients. Because of confidentiality it wasn't appropriate for me to tell him anything, but I didn't know how to handle the situation. I knew I needed to be prepared for this meeting, but all I could do, all I could see, all I could feel, was how awful the meeting was going to be. I could imagine him as he'd been before, saying; 'You've got to tell me. It's all very well, but I'm in charge of this college, I'm responsible.' And that was all that was in my mind. I could imagine myself shrinking in my chair in front of him. Not a pretty sight. You can imagine how I walked into the room, not with my head held high. I shuffled in, sat down in a chair and waited. Waited for a bad time. Thankfully it wasn't as bad or as awful as I'd thought it was going to be, but it wasn't very pleasant and I didn't enjoy having to say to him, 'I'm not going to tell you.'

As I recall it now, I think about the amount of energy and time I wasted worrying about the situation. I probably spent up to fifteen minutes before the meeting doing nothing except worrying about what I was going to say to him. And I probably spent up to a day before that thinking about how I was going to have to see him and have an unpleasant experience.

Does that sound familiar to you? If it does, then just think about how often you set yourself up for failure. And how often you set yourself up for success. Because we're doing it to ourselves, no-one else is doing it to us. I often think we don't need anyone else to criticize us or shout at us, we do it so well for ourselves. But what we can do instead is choose whether we're going to dwell on the negatives in our mind and our body or think more positively and become more active. While I was worrying about going to see him, I wasn't doing anything else.

Your turn

Remember a time when you've worried about doing something you haven't wanted to do, or you've been nervous or anxious about something. How have you prepared yourself? Did you think: 'Well, this is one meeting. I can handle it, I know what's going on here'? Or did you think, 'Oh it's going to be awful. It's going to be as bad as it was last time', or 'I don't know how bad it's going to be, but I know it's going to be bad', or 'Everybody's told me I can't expect anything from him', or 'She's always going to shout, you know what she's like.' And if you make those sort of statements, just think about what's going on inside your body. Is it a lovely log-cabin sort of sensation, or is it something much worse? Perhaps you're out in the cold in the snow and you haven't got a coat on. I believe that you get what you focus on, so it's important to think about what you want and how you want to achieve it.

35

Question

What holds you back?

Just for a moment, think about the sorts of things that you say to yourself that perhaps hold you back from doing something you want to do but feel nervous about, or hold you back from doing something you don't particularly want to do but you know you have to get on with. What sorts of things do you say to yourself and what effect do they have on you? What do you do?

If I go back to my situation with the principal, I realize that I was telling myself, 'I really don't want to go in. I probably haven't got time to talk to him properly. He's never going to believe me. What if he shouts? What if he forces me?' All these sorts of things were going on in my mind. I felt uncomfortable, I felt uncertain and I felt that he had the upper hand – which of course I'd given him! I felt confused, I felt awkward, and part of what I was saying was 'I don't want to go there, I don't want to be there.' What did I do? Well, very little really. Just sat, worried and waited until the 'dreaded' time for the appointment.

Change your language

What sorts of things do you say to yourself, and how do you feel after you've said them? I wonder if you say something like 'Well, they'll think I'm stupid', 'I'm not going to enjoy it', 'I haven't got enough time', 'It won't be any good', 'I'll make a fool of myself.' Any of these statements will just stop you from taking any action.

Sometimes the things that we say to ourselves are the things that other people used to say to us, and again you have a choice about whether to accept them now. Notice, and maybe note down, the sorts of things that you say to yourself to stop yourself from doing something or that engage you in lots of worrying time. Once you've written down the list of what you say, then write down how you feel and what effect those words have on you. It could be something like you feel insecure, you feel inadequate, you feel horrible, you feel negative, you feel intimidated or anxious. These are not helpful feelings, and yet they're feelings we're imposing on ourselves.

When you feel these feelings, what do you do and how do you act? Very often, what you do is absolutely nothing. You can almost become paralysed by your negative feelings. Taken to its extreme, that's what depression is. When you get depressed you become lethargic, you become inert and you can't do anything because all your energy is going inwards into thinking the negative thoughts. So just imagine how it would be if you changed those thoughts. Instead of saying 'They'll think I'm stupid', what else could you say? 'I know I'm not stupid, I'm interested to know what they think.' If you say things like 'I don't have enough time', 'I'm too busy', then I would check with yourself what it is you're really saying, because sometimes that's an excuse. It's not that you don't have enough time, it's that you tend to do the things you want to do. Start noticing what you do have time for. And if you're faced with something you don't want to do, admit it. That is a more positive and clear statement from which you can make some decisions. You may still have to do it, but at least you're active and not wasting time with excuses.

You can change your attitude by changing your language. Instead of 'I've forgotten', say 'I will remember soon.' Instead of 'It's a problem', which needs time to find a solution, or 'I'll sort it', say 'It's a nuisance or a challenge', which doesn't need fixing and frees you time to sort it out.

Use the table below to make changes to your language which will alter how you feel and what you do as a result.

Tell myself	Feelings	Actions	Change to
It will be awful. I'll get it wrong.	Inadequate, scared, stupid.	Do nothing, keep putting it off, make excuses.	I'll have a go. What's the worst thing that can happen?
I can't ...	Helpless, hopeless.	Avoid or withdraw.	There's plenty I can do. I'll do what I can.

Question

What do you talk about at the end of a day?

How often do you go home from work, or at the end of your day, sit down and say to anyone who is listening, 'Let me tell you about the best thing that happened to me today', or 'Do you know, there was one really great thing that happened to me today'? I guess not very

37

often. Perhaps you recognize this scene better: you go home and you say, 'You'll never believe the day I had today! I tell you, everything that could have gone wrong went wrong.' Think about the tone of your voice, the feelings and your body language when you say that sort of thing.

If this hasn't been your best ever day, do you want to make sure you have a rotten night too? Do you want to carry the clutter around so you can stay in a bad mood and bring everyone else down, or let go and enjoy whatever you can? To do this you can start by noticing the 'nuggets of gold' that happen to you during your day – the little things that make you smile as well as the great big ones that make you jump for joy. Record them in some way every day, as the following table, for example. They could be part of your 'success log', too. It may seem a bit strange at first. Persevere and you will have a collection that will inspire you.

Nuggets collection	Week beginning . . .
Day 1	
Day 2	
Day 3	
Day 4	
Day 5	
Day 6	
Day 7	

Brian was amazed at the idea that he could have some control over the thoughts which led to his negative feelings and resulted in inaction or, even worse, sleepless nights. We worked on noticing when these happened and how he could stop them and put them aside. He runs a weekly keep-fit class at the local leisure centre and it is usually well attended. Recently, after a two-week break, he returned to his class and only three people turned up. Brian was mortified and began his negative-thinking routine. 'They preferred the guy who took over in my place, they've gone to his sessions. They've realized I'm no good.' He noticed immediately what he was doing to himself and decided to change the message. 'There is probably a logical explanation. I'll check with the centre before I leave. I can ring the missing people and find out what stopped them coming.' He was able to work with the three who did turn up and concentrate on the class rather than on his own distress. At the end of the session he discovered that the centre had been telling people there was no session that evening and the three who turned up had done so independently. Brian was delighted on two counts. First, the lack of participants was down to misinformation, not his inadequacies, and second, he had a great night's sleep.

Popular sayings

Think about the sayings like 'You mustn't get too big for your boots', 'Don't blow your own trumpet' and 'Pride comes before a fall'. In Shift 2 it was apparent that we are handed these and many other phrases by parents, people in authority and society in general. They then become internalized and we find ourselves repeating them at times when we think we are in danger of becoming big-headed or 'too pleased' with ourselves. Maybe they are there to make sure we keep ourselves in check and that we don't overstep the mark. I would like to encourage you to think about overstepping your mark and notice what happens to you. It is unlikely that you will be shunned by everyone you know and be destroyed on the spot. And yet there is something inside our heads that makes us fearful of rebelling in this way. I challenge you to read your 'nuggets of gold' and acknowledge them to yourself and others. You can start using your own sayings that work for you.

Moment of choice

Think about something that you're going to do that you're not looking forward to and that you've already spent time worrying about. Start focusing now on how well it could go, on the best thing that could happen and the outcome you want. Choose to help yourself feel more relaxed and in charge.

In my situation with the college principal, I could have handled the time before the meeting very differently and made the interview a lot easier. I could have said to myself, 'OK, I know the sort of thing he's going to talk about. He wants some information, and from my professional point of view it's not appropriate for me to give him that information. How can I get him to accept that? He's a reasonable chap, I know what my boundaries are and I know what I want to say. Let's think about how I can handle this in such a way that I feel comfortable and he feels comfortable.' This would have made a huge difference. Then I would have pictured myself going in there with my head held high, sitting down and knowing what I wanted to say and being very clear. It would probably have taken me a maximum of ten minutes' mental preparation, rather than many hours' worrying.

The key thing I had to learn was that *he* wasn't doing anything to me, *I* was doing it to myself. He wasn't there when I was having all the awful thoughts. I was creating them. It was my choice.

Perform the impossible

> Whether you think you can or whether you think you can't, you're probably right.
>
> (Henry Ford)

I love to read and hear stories about people who have achieved impossible feats against all odds or achieved lifetime ambitions despite everyone else telling them they couldn't.

A prime example is the athlete Roger Bannister. For years nobody could run a four-minute mile; it just wasn't possible. They got almost there but they couldn't quite make it. Bannister decided to train his mind alongside his muscles to manage the impossible. He conditioned himself to believe that the four-minute mile was achievable, even though no-one else agreed. Others thought of it as a barrier, he considered it a gateway to many other records and opportunities. And, of course, he was right. The fascinating part is that after he had broken the record many others did, too. Once they knew it could be done, of course they could do it. But somebody had to be the first. Somebody had to believe it, to dream it, to feel it and go out and do it. And that somebody was Roger Bannister.

We know about parents who perform amazing acts of strength and courage to rescue their children. They don't stop to think, 'I can't possibly lift that car', they just get on and do it. Only afterwards are they aware of the enormity of what they have done and call it a fluke. They will not be able to repeat the action under 'normal' conditions, because they will be thinking about all the reasons that make it impossible. It is the same with 'beginners' luck'. The first time round you have nothing to measure against and nothing to lose. Once you have been successful, the doubting thoughts can creep in to stop success from becoming a habit. You start to tell yourself, 'I'll never do that well again' or 'I can't believe I did so well.' And guess what happens? . . .

Question

Who inspires you and how can you inspire yourself?

What are the 'can do's' in your life? Achievers focus on their successes. They tell themselves how well they have done and enjoy their achievements. When things don't go according to plan they work out the learning and accept that they can redeem something from the situation. Think about the people whose lives inspire you. They may be dead or alive, strangers or friends. What can you learn from them and how do you think they would handle any of your challenging situations?

If what you think is what you get, then focus your thinking to keep the positives uppermost. You need to focus on the times you've done well and talk to yourself as a successful person. Create a list of everything that you have ever achieved in your life, even including learning to walk and talk. Aim for as many as you can. Remember that many things that are automatic now were once immensely challenging. Add to your list every day and enjoy your successes.

> Did is a word of achievement,
> Won't is a word of retreat,
> Might is a word of bereavement,
> Can't is a word of defeat,
> Ought is a word of duty,
> Try is a word each hour,
> Will is a word of beauty,
> Can is a word of power.
>
> (Anonymous)

Shift 5
Create more confidence

I was always looking outside myself for strength and confidence but it comes from within. It is there all the time.
(Anna Freud, psychoanalyst and youngest daughter of Sigmund Freud)

One can choose to go back toward safety or forward to growth. Growth must be chosen again and again; fear must be overcome again and again.
(Abraham Maslow, psychologist)

Low confidence or low self-esteem are at the root of most of the issues I deal with as a coach, trainer and counsellor. I know that most of us are able to and do achieve many things of which we are proud. Often, though, we dismiss them because they seem so 'simple' or because, having achieved them, we forget the trials and tribulations on the way. Or, even worse for our self-esteem, we think they must be a fluke and quickly resign them to a place in our minds where we can ignore them. When we feel good about ourselves we expect things to work and go well for us; when we don't we are only open to disasters and failure.

Self-esteem is essential to our well-being and is something that can grow or diminish, depending on what is happening in our lives. It can come from either internal or external sources. For some of us the external influences are the greater, which means that we think we are dependent on those around us or the community at large to assess our value. This is fine when those around us appreciate and give us the positive feedback we require for a healthy self-esteem. But if we lose their approval or support we can feel worthless and useless.

Question

Is your self-esteem and confidence mainly dependent on the approval and opinions of others?

If the answer is sometimes 'yes', look at the list in the 'external self-esteem tower' below and decide where the positive opinions come from and where the negatives. Which are good for your self-esteem and which are not? What, if anything, has a positive impact on your self-esteem and is worth retaining? Add any sources that are missing for you.

External self-esteem tower

Source	Positive or negative	Retain
Awards		
Praise		
Work colleagues		
Job – promotion		
Job – status		
Qualifications		
Other significant adults		
Own children		
Partner		
Teachers		
Friends		
Family members		
Brothers and sisters		
Parents		

When bits of this tower disappear we can feel unresourceful. It is shaky and can fall down around us. Any one of the sources can be withdrawn deliberately or through 'natural attrition'. If you lose your job and all your sense of self is associated with it, then you will feel as though you have few resources and little confidence to move on. If your family breaks up and your total identity has depended on your role as a parent, you may feel lost and aimless.

It is crucial to examine how you fare in the internal self-esteem stakes. If your balance is low, then now is the time to consider ways of boosting your morale from within.

Moment of choice

Internal self-esteem is yours any and all of the time you choose to accept and nurture it.

If you put your energies into building up your 'internal self-esteem tower' (below) you can increase your self-belief and feel more confident. Only you can remove the blocks from your tower and, equally, only you can add to it and enhance your resources. As our internal self-esteem develops, we become far less dependent on others for approval. We develop trust in our own instincts and feelings, learning to truly love and appreciate ourselves.

In the table below are some ideas for strengthening your 'internal self-esteem tower'. Add more now and as you carry on enjoying being you in your life.

Everyone has a moment in their past when they have been successful and done something outstanding.

(Black, 1992)

Internal self-esteem tower

Love yourself
Let go of comparisons
Treat yourself like your best friend
Respect yourself and others
Reward yourself – paint, read, sing, bathe, exercise, meditate, etc.
Look after yourself
Be kind to yourself – stop giving yourself a hard time
Accept compliments
Stop self put-downs
Recognize your knowledge
Acknowledge your skills
Forgive yourself and others
Know your strengths
Self-praise

No comparisons

It would be hard to name a more certain sign of poor self-esteem than the need to perceive some other group as inferior.

(Branden, 1995)

We can confuse self-esteem and feeling good with feeling superior. Unfortunately, in order to feel superior we depend on comparing ourselves with someone who, by definition, becomes inferior. Sometimes there is no-one with whom to make this comparison and our fragile superiority falls down. We may just as easily decide to compare ourselves with others so that we are the ones feeling inferior, which then confirms our 'I'm no good' feelings about ourselves.

Start right now to approve of yourself unconditionally and keep your mind in positive mode. Live for now and act, rather than waiting for the 'right time', because it may never arrive. Begin by being less judgemental of yourself and others. While we are focused on comparisons we lose a true sense of self.

Question

Have you ever compared yourself to anyone else? And have you ever come out equal?

We used to have a very well-trained and beautifully behaved border collie. She was 'Miss Perfect'. She didn't need a lead and would stay 'to heel' whatever the provocation. It was easy to feel smug and superior as other people were dragged along by their misbehaving pooches. On the arrival of our new border collie things changed. She is much naughtier, pulls on the lead and has been known to run off after a fascinating scent leaving me hoarse and embarrassed in the middle of the field. Not so superior now, eh? I am sure others look pityingly as I try to control this whirlwind of free spirit. The point is that from both sides I missed the opportunity to work with my dogs individually and enhance their unique characters. I was so busy wanting to be 'best' and comparing my performance with other people's that I wasn't enjoying the relationship for its own sake.

I learned that even feeling superior is a somewhat hollow feeling, and while it is dependent on someone else for comparison it can easily disappear. I was then introduced to the notion of 'equal and different', a concept that is now central to all the personal development work I do. The most rewarding way to think about ourselves and other people is to consider us all in the most general way that puts everyone on an equal footing. This means treating everyone as an equal human being with individual differences. Everyone has different strengths and limitations that have developed throughout their lives and in response to the many incidents they have encountered. If you focus on others who have the attributes that you lack and long for, then you will feel inferior and short-changed. This feeling of deficiency, even in one area, has a negative impact on your self-esteem. When you start to think of everyone as a human being then we all become equal. Tall, short, rich, poor, knowledge-able, ignorant – whatever category you choose all becomes irrelevant. We are all human beings and there becomes no need for comparisons or judgements. We don't need to put others down to feel good about ourselves or use others' qualities to beat ourselves up.

We all have areas that could be improved in our lives and areas in which we excel. Our self-esteem is affected by how we chose to relate to them. We should celebrate our differences. Our uniqueness is part of what makes each one of us special. Can you recall any family sayings based on comparisons – e.g. 'You'll never be as ... as your brother/sister/mother/father'? Or 'Why can't you be more like Auntie Sashia, she is always there when you need her?' Reconsider and decide whether they are useful or limiting compari-sons. If they are unhelpful, let them go, and reconfirm: 'I am me and I'm great the way I am.'

Moment of choice

Next time you find yourself indulging in comparison with another person or group of people, stop and ask yourself, 'Is this to make me feel better or worse about myself?' Whichever it is, stop, and decide how to nurture yourself so that you feel OK as you are. Then remember 'equal and different'. This will make a huge difference to you and to your relationships with others.

> Bruno was unhappy being on his own. It seemed as if everyone else was in a relationship. He felt inferior and wondered what was wrong with him. We decided he had three options: to go and do something, anything, to change the situation; to stay as he was and still feel unhappy and uncomfortable (which might lead to someone taking him on out of pity); or to stay the way he was, but stop the comparisons and change the way he thought and felt about it. There were many benefits to him as a single person and he could choose to focus on those instead.

The fear factor
When self-esteem is low, it is often the by-product of fear. Our fears block success, happiness and achievement and keep us in a 'no good' place.

The solution is in the mind. As we step into the fear it disappears:

we feel so much better for having taken some action and, in most cases, we realize that the situation wasn't that bad after all. We noted in Shift 3 how much time we waste worrying about how bad something might be, and in the same way we use up time and energy avoiding things because we are afraid of the outcome. You'll never know until you have a go.

I was talking to a group about the fears that hold them back, and one woman told how she and her husband had split up amicably some time ago. Now he wanted to try again. She was torn and thought it best not to 'in case things went wrong again. They might be worse than they are now.' Not surprisingly, I countered with, 'and they may be even better. If you go back and it doesn't work you'll know and be able to move on. If you don't, you may spend time wondering how it would have been.'

When people talk about preferring the 'devil' they know, they are keeping themselves low on self-esteem and in an uncomfortable place. I prefer

> You would take drastic steps to get rid of any poison that found its way into your food. So let it be with fear, the mind poison.
>
> (Hill, 1998)

Question

And what would be the worst thing?

Whenever you find yourself held back by the fear factor, ask yourself: what would be the worst thing? And then ask it again and again until you come to realize that it's very unlikely that your fears will lead to the end of the world (yours or the complete universe's). Not asking that question is what is scaring you subconsciously.

I wanted to challenge Freya's assumptions around perfection and lack of self-respect. She has lived her life following an image she thinks other people expect from her. I kept asking her:

Q   What would be the worst thing if you didn't exercise all the time, or your stomach wasn't flat?
R   People would think I was fat.
Q   And what would be the worst thing about that?
R   They would think I'm a slob.
Q   And what would be the worst thing about that?
R   That would mean I have no self-control.

Q   And what would be the worst thing about that?
R   I wouldn't fit my image.
Q   And what would be the worst thing about that?
R   They wouldn't want to be with me.
Q   And what would be the worst thing about that?
R   I can't cope with knowing I've let everyone down.
Q   And what would be the worst thing about that?
R   OK, I give up.

By continuously answering the question, Freya eventually ran out of ideas and realized that it wouldn't be the end of the world if she didn't exercise so fanatically. We discussed the notion that 'nobody's perfect and who wants to be nobody?'

This technique is sometimes called 'root cause audit' because it encourages you to move from the first, reasoned response, to the heart of the issue. It's what children are doing when they keep asking 'why'. They want to understand things at a deeper level than we are sometimes able or willing to explain.

What do we fear? We may fear 'reality', because we feel inadequate, or exposure, humiliation, failure, letting ourselves or others down, or vulnerability. Sometimes we are fearful of success and the responsibilities which accompany it. We are frightened of being 'found out' to be less than we think people think we are. How complicated we make things for ourselves. Fear has been described as 'false expectation appearing real' – a way of wasting time on worrying about the unknown future. In the worst cases we learn to sabotage our potential and keep ourselves 'in our place', rather than shine. If we perform better or appear happier than those around us, we might be disliked or rejected.

Pride

I recently attended a show celebrating the International Day of Disabled People. It was a very moving event on a number of levels and greatly related to issues of self-esteem. First there were artists making music via computers, using various parts of their bodies to push the keys. They were accompanied by wheelchair dancers, who wheeled themselves or were pushed and pulled around the stage to great effect. They moved gracefully and with a great sense of performance. They were grinning from ear to ear and obviously greatly enjoying the moment. The next act was a deaf person signing to songs – a sign language version of karaoke. This was one of the most moving acts I have ever seen. Although he could not hear the words, he had learned them and put all this experience of life into the performance. Finally, came an activist with a guitar. He was in a wheelchair, and his main song was about pride and disability. He prefaced it by saying that being disabled was just another way of being and that if you were proud of yourself as a human being and recognized what you had to offer the world you could treat yourself with respect and gain respect from others. A very powerful experience.

Boasting

For some of you, just seeing the heading 'Boasting' may cause you to cringe or come out in a cold sweat. I am sure that will be a temporary response if this book is doing its job properly. If you cannot admit your strengths and positive characteristics to yourself, how can you expect to be open to others' praise either? When people are asked to fill in a questionnaire about their strengths and weaknesses, they jokingly ask for extra paper for the weaknesses and struggle to write anything on the strengths page. We may laugh but it isn't funny. We are so uncomfortable with the thought that we may excel in some areas of our lives and daren't talk about them in case we break the spell or are 'found out'.

'If people knew the real me they wouldn't be so fulsome in their praise. They think I know my stuff, but that's a façade.' When Jake said that to me I had to laugh. 'If you're managing to fool them and they are benefiting from your so-called knowledge you must be even cleverer than they think you are.' This was not the response he wanted from me. He would much rather I had agreed and endorsed his self put-down.

Jake is typical of the people I meet who are highly talented and yet don't recognize it. Their successes are always a shock and they are unable to own their part in them. I think it is very sad that he and people like him are unable to appreciate themselves in the same way as others. It is much more fun to do something and know inside that you are doing it well rather than having to depend on others' approval, and even then not believing them.

Blowing your trumpet

When you are content to be simply yourself and don't compare or compete, everybody will respect you.

(Lao-Tzu)

Remember in Shift 1 I asked you to think about the goals you have in the various aspects of your life? I would now like you to revisit these areas. Use the table below to collect as many positive statements as you can about your skills and abilities in these areas. It is so important to realize that much of what we do 'automatically' had to be learned once (or on many occasions) and that skills from everyday life can be transferred and valued in the world of work, and vice versa.

Social life (e.g. negotiating) _____
Relationships (e.g. keeping in
  touch with faraway friends) _____
Family (e.g. resolving
  conflict, teaching, team-building) _____
Finances (e.g. budgeting,
  housekeeping) _____
Work (e.g. motivating,
  skill with technology) _____
Living space (e.g. creativity
  with colour, painting) _____
Leisure (e.g. sport, design) _____
Health (e.g. nutrition) _____
Retirement (e.g. forward planning) _____
Spiritual life (e.g. relaxing,
  meditating) _____
Communications (e.g. listening,
  problem-solving) _____

Remember to focus on the things you can do rather than the things you can't.

Check whether you felt the need to qualify your attributes with a 'quite or not bad'. If so, strike those out and leave the statements to stand alone. This is not a time for false modesty but one for honest self-appreciation. There are some things at which you excel. *Admit it*.

Only me

Saying 'only me' and 'I'm just a . . .' are part of everyday speech and may not seem to have much impact. On a subconscious level they have a lessening effect on you and your self-esteem. Your subconscious is taking in a negative message that it adds to the 'no good' collection and takes at face value. They say our subconsciouses don't have a sense of humour and aren't aware that these throwaway self-insults are meant to be jokes. When people ring me up and say, 'It's only me,' I'm sometimes tempted to say, 'Well, in that case I won't bother talking to you.'

The new MD of a very prestigious car company was quick to stop any talk of 'just a' throughout the firm. He would regularly lecture on the business school circuit and told how one of his most important employees was the man who cleaned the factory floor. When visitors walked around the plant, they always commented on the clean floors in busy technical areas. They felt confident in the company and the image of care that went with it.

Write down or record everything you do well, are proud of and have achieved in your own 'feel good' book. It'll be there when you don't feel so good, to remind you of those wonderful unique talents that you have.

At one 'boasting' session, Petra was describing her proudest moment. She told how she had trained to run a half marathon that would end with a lap round the Crystal Palace stadium. She was not a natural runner and knew it would be a huge challenge for her. Embarrassed and yet undeterred, she went ahead, and realized that she was last and the only person still running when she entered the stadium. Petra was pleased with herself to have stayed the course. Imagine her delight when the whole stadium gave her a standing ovation as she ran slowly round the last lap to complete her race. She treasures that moment as a triumph of her spirit.

Compliments

Now you have conquered your concerns about self-appreciation, it's time to think about others' words of admiration. It's great to be able to take compliments and have them boost your external self-esteem tower when they are a reinforcement of your own self-worth. I certainly prefer to accept a compliment rather than agonize over the hidden meaning or catch. Just as we are not schooled in the art of giving criticism in a way that it can be heard, so we are not taught how to compliment people. The result is that sometimes a genuine compliment sounds hackneyed or awkward, and if the recipient is unsure of themselves, they will automatically take it as insincere.

I was working with the staff of a police force and we were discussing feedback. One of the delegates talked about his inspector, who had been on a management course and came back into the office and complimented him on the previous week's activities. This apparently new and unexpected behaviour prompted the constable to reply; 'Well, I was just doing my job' and to think, 'What's she after?' The manager was probably left thinking, 'Well, that was a waste of time, I'll not bother again.' Neither of them was pleased with the interaction, and could find no benefit. I suggested to the constable that he give the inspector a chance to practise her new behaviour and enjoy the fact that someone appreciated that he was doing his job and doing it well. I even suggested the constable think about any genuine, positive statements he could make to the inspector, and realize how challenging it can be when that is not the norm of the organization.

Think about your most common response to compliments. Do you

- Throw back praise like a hot potato:
  'Oh, this old thing, I've had it years' – then you'll never get to feel its benefit.
- Use it for comparison:
  'It's not as good as yours' – they'll feel less inclined to say anything and may feel embarrassed or confused.
- Point out what they've missed:
  'There are three typos on page 5' – they'll think you're not listening, not interested or not receptive, so won't bother again.
- Disagree
  – they'll feel offended and put down.

In the worst case, they could even take your response as an insult, telling them they don't know what they're talking about.

Question

Who compliments you and who do you pay compliments to? Use the table below to look at your behaviour.

Receive from . . . When and how . . . Reaction . . . Give to . . . Reaction

---

When I was working as a college counsellor I once commented to my external supervisor that I felt unappreciated. No-one ever told me what they thought of the job I was doing. (Note the need there for external self-esteem.) She shrewdly asked me how many other staff I talked to and acknowledged their contribution to the college. Point taken. It hadn't occurred to me that as I sat waiting for some feedback I was simply exacerbating my isolation and probably seemed self-sufficient to the 'outside world'. Needless to say, once I ventured out and took the risk of talking to others about their role in the college I started to receive some fascinating and useful feedback.

Someone has to make the first move: why not let it be you? If you receive a frosty or suspicious response to early compliments, remember that if this is new behaviour it may be challenging for the recipients. Persevere, and you'll all benefit in the end. It is lovely to give a sincere compliment that is accepted and believed.

Moment of choice

Next time anyone pays you a compliment, choose to accept it graciously and say thank you. Notice your initial reaction and check why you might want to disown the praise. Then acknowledge it to yourself and think how you might add to it.

Yes, I really enjoyed it.
It took ages and I'm glad it's worked out well.
It's good when things come together.
Yes, it does suit me.

- Ask your friends, family, children, colleagues or partner to pay you genuine compliments and practise saying thank you. Resist the urge to give the compliments back. Write them down and enjoy re-reading them.
- Pay compliments to other people and don't expect anything back. Don't be surprised if you get a strange reaction. Sometimes the reason people don't pay compliments is because we don't give them – so someone has to set the ball rolling.
- If you want to qualify a thank you, always do it in a positive way. It's no good saying thank you if you're going to add an 'it wasn't hard' at the end.

Shift 6

Behave yourself

Two thousand years ago the Roman philosopher Cicero considered that the six states below could contribute to an individual's downfall:

1 the delusion that personal gain is made by crushing others;
2 the tendency to worry about things that cannot be changed or corrected;
3 insisting that a thing is impossible because we cannot accomplish it;
4 refusing to set aside trivial preferences;
5 neglecting development and refinement of the mind and not acquiring the habit of reading and studying;
6 attempting to compel others to believe and live as we do.

It seems to me that in some aspects we haven't moved very far in the intervening years. For some reason we can tend to hang on to unhelpful beliefs, attitudes and behaviours. Very often the biggest catch is that we believe the way we behave is beyond our control and is a result of the way we have been treated or taught in the past. While we function from this base, we are indeed helpless and reliant on others for the lead. We can swing from extremes of passively allowing others to walk all over us, so as to keep the peace, to explosive outbursts of aggression.

Moment of choice

If we stop long enough to think about it, we can choose how we react and behave in any situation. Otherwise, and particularly when we feel pressured, we tend to respond as we have habitually done in the past, and usually with the same unsatisfactory results. The choices are those of:

- *Surrendering ourselves* – My friend consistently keeps me waiting. I pluck up courage to say how much of an inconvenience it is. He starts to tell me his trials and tribulations and I say 'sorry' for adding to them. The pattern continues. I feel angry with myself and with him, but dare not repeat my outburst in case he decides he doesn't want to be my friend any longer. Anyway, I should put others' needs before mine.

- *Attacking the other person* – My friend consistently keeps me waiting. I have had enough and I let rip. 'Have you any idea how inconsiderate and self-centred you are? You are a ****** liability. Don't think I'll wait for you again.' He either joins in the slanging match or slopes off, wondering how to redeem things. I feel justified at first and then feel a sense of shame at my elaborate outburst.

- *Undermining indirectly* – My friend consistently keeps me waiting. I'm not happy about it and not quite sure what to do. I tell our mutual friend and hope that she sorts it for me, or I say, 'Good of you to turn up. I've got quite used to my own company.' He may laugh it off or just ignore it. I have to hope that my strong sense of disapproval and injustice has been picked up with the little barb to sting him.

There is an effective alternative – assertive behaviour – which enables us to take much greater charge of our lives, relax and do things in a constructive way.

- *Clearly state our needs and understand theirs* – My friend consistently keeps me waiting.

  1 I decide to talk to him about it when we both have time for the discussion.

It is very important to find time to talk when you are both calm. If you react in the heat of the moment you are more likely to fuel the fire. If you wait until you are both receptive you give yourself a better chance of a beneficial discussion.

  2 I tell him, 'I get cheesed off when you turn up late, it sets the whole evening off badly. I want to be pleased to see you, not cursing you. How can we sort it out?'

By describing the behaviour and how I feel about it, I am letting him hear my genuine emotions. I am also asking for his help to resolve things. The key is to defuse the situation first and create a climate that fosters a discussion rather than a battle. So often, a bit of give and take on both sides can save a potentially explosive situation.

3 He may explain the constraints he has and we can consider them, or we may agree to meet somewhere where I can wait comfortably until he arrives.

We've at least started talking, and that's three-quarters of the way towards a solution.

Sometimes people are really surprised to think that there is actually a choice in the way they behave. You can choose to behave non-assertively and understand what that means, or choose to behave assertively and feel more in control of yourself and better able to handle things constructively. For me, assertiveness is a way of behaving that facilitates relationships. It's a way of creating win–win situations and can enhance communications in many cases at home or at work.

Figure 1 shows these four types of behaviour.

If we look at each of the behaviours in more detail it becomes clear that they are not as simple as they might first seem. Each of the non-assertive behaviours has been a coping behaviour in the past. By that I mean that when we are children we may not be encouraged to be assertive or express our opinions and feelings, so we have to find another way to declare them. We learn what 'works', brings us attention and meets our needs. This behaviour becomes habitual. As we mature we sometimes are unaware that the assertive alternative exists and can create better feelings all around us. We stay stuck in our old, habitual responses, particularly when we feel pressured.

Maisie grew up in a large family. The youngest of five, she found the most effective way of getting attention was to throw a tantrum. Her elder siblings were often reprimanded and she was cuddled. Great while it lasted. She was miserable at school when this behaviour didn't work. Later on she was constantly changing relationships because no-one wanted to live with Maisie and her temper.

Fergus grew up in an abusive family. He was often beaten for getting things wrong or refusing to do anything he was asked to do. Not surprisingly he found the best way of coping was to keep his head down, say as little as possible and hope he wouldn't be noticed. He was considered 'shy' and simple at school but did not dare to offer his views even if he knew they were valid. As he grew up he was often bullied and put upon. He felt his potential was never recognized.

Dai's behaviour was more complex. He quickly learned that the way to succeed was to flatter or manipulate those around him. He learned how to hit the guilt buttons in people. His skill was in deceiving others and, ultimately, deceiving himself. He wouldn't risk the direct approach like Maisie because he didn't trust either himself or anyone else. His sarcasm was sharp and amusing unless you happened to be the one on the receiving end. People were very wary of him and felt unable to trust most things he said.

Ghislaine was brought up believing that she had a contribution to make to her family and was encouraged to express her opinions and feelings. She learned early on about straightforward compromise and negotiation. She had respect for herself and respect for others. She was able to recognize and accept both her positive and her negative qualities. She was good to be with because people knew where they stood with her.

It is important to note that none of us fits into only one or two of these behaviours all the time to the exclusion of the others. We all behave in each of these ways some of the time. We need to recognize that this is also the case for those around us. I used to work with a boss whom I would have said was aggressive full stop. Yet looking back I can think of times when she behaved passively and let herself be put upon by company directors, or indirectly when she would talk about other staff members behind their backs, to be 'one of the girls'. She behaved assertively when she calmly defended her staff and ensured that we were represented in the wider aspects of company policy.

Through my training I also learned not to label people 'passive' or 'assertive', but to describe them as behaving in that way. This is crucial to the way we relate to people. Once you have labelled them, their whole being can become connected to that label and you fail to consider them in any other way. If you are simply describing their behaviour, then this is something that can easily be different on different occasions. Of course, they may have you labelled in one of the boxes – which would it be?

Question

When do you behave assertively or non-assertively? Does it depend on the circumstances or the people? Use the table below to look at how you act.

Behaviour	Who with?	Type of situation?	What do you do?
Assertive			
Passive			
Indirect			
Aggressive			

You might want to check out with your friends and colleagues how they perceive your behaviour. Beware of your response. If you don't like what you hear, remember it is their opinion, which you requested, and it is worth considering. If they say you can be aggressive sometimes and you furiously deny it, you may just be proving them right.

Power plays

One of the key areas in which you can recognize the different behaviours is in the way that people use or misuse power.

When I behave assertively the power is coming from within me, so it's an internal power. I feel confident, with strong internal self-esteem and respect for myself and others. I believe that we are equal and different in the way we relate to the world. I will take action rather than wait to react to others and I will take responsibility for myself instead of blaming others. I value the other person(s) with whom I am interacting and want to understand their perception of things. I have respect for myself and I have respect for them.

When I behave in an aggressive way I'm using my power to have power over others, which takes away any equality in a relationship. My hollow victory comes from belittling the thoughts, values and capabilities of others. I must win at all costs. This, of course, often indicates how fragile my self-esteem is. I need to be right to feel OK about myself. Or I need to know that when I am putting you down, I am assured of being 'top dog', if only momentarily.

When I behave passively, I give my power up to other people and so the equality is in a different imbalance. Given the opportunity I will opt out of making a decision or a criticism or offering an opinion. I either submit or run away. I am so concerned to keep the peace or ensure a quiet life that I suppress my needs for the 'greater good'. I am constantly wanting approval and won't confront something or someone I don't like.

When I behave indirectly I misuse my power to control others and in some cases to foster dependency. I may take excessive care of someone so that I am indispensable and they become 'helpless'. Or I may use emotional blackmail to control a situation without directly stating my needs or requirements. I try to bring others into my circle to support my criticism of someone else who never directly hears a bad word from me.

Below is a collection of situations which could result in any of the different types of behaviour. Think about which would be the closest to your most likely response. Take some time to think why you and others behave in these ways and what the effects are. In future you might choose to respond differently now you have some new ideas.

Moment of choice

Remember, you can choose how you behave if you stop and count to five before acting or opening your mouth. Also notice that the way you say things and the tone you use can signal different behaviours.

Social situations

In a restaurant if your food is cold:

- *Aggressive* – Loudly demand to see the manager and make sure as many people as possible are watching. Then lay into her and generalize one cold dish to the complete workings of the restaurant. Your companions will either cheer you on or try to slink away, totally embarrassed by your outburst.
- *Passive* – Either say nothing and suffer, or say, 'Yes, everything's lovely', if asked how it is. Could possibly then move into . . .
- *Indirect* – Mutter to your companions, and anyone else who'll listen, about the poor service and be sure to tell others not to go there because the food is cold. If the waiter asks how the meal is you answer 'Fine', leave a pause and then, just as they turn away, 'if you like eating sawdust'.
- *Assertive* – Use your understanding first to be able to talk to the waiter. You know they're busy, and unfortunately your food is cold. You would appreciate a replacement.

You want to complain about an item that you have recently bought:

- *Aggressive* – I am disgusted at the quality of this item. You should be ashamed of yourself at thinking of selling such things. Give me a refund, now.
- *Passive* – I don't want to bother you and I know it's not your fault. But I don't think this is working quite as it should. Maybe I've not connected it properly, but I'd appreciate it if you'd just check. I'd quite like a refund please, if it's at all possible.
- *Indirect* – I suppose I was daft to expect anything better from a store like yours. Still we can always hope. I'm sure you'll want to give me a full refund to save any bad publicity or solicitors' letters.
- *Assertive* – I wonder if you can help me. I'd be so pleased if we could sort this out. I bought this last week and it doesn't work. (If you wait for their response you may well have it sorted without needing to ask for a refund, though you can have that in reserve.)

Relationships

It's your birthday and you know exactly what you want. It's not what others are likely to buy you:

- *Aggressive* – I've decided what I want for my birthday and you'd better buy it or your life won't be worth living.
- *Passive* – Say nothing, dream and resign yourself to the fact that you'll get the same sort of gift as before.
- *Indirect* – Drop hints and leave a number of strategically ringed adverts around the house.
- *Assertive* – Disclose your feelings that you have found the gift you really want. Tell the appropriate person or people that you would be thrilled to have it and where they can find it.

Your partner's parents are coming to stay for the weekend. You know that their mother will find fault with you and make sarcastic comments for a large portion of the time, perhaps even mentioning your predecessor and how efficient and organized they were:

- *Aggressive* – Hit back with as many rude things as you can think of about the mother. Play her at her own game.
- *Passive* – Feel hurt and wounded. Put yourself down with the thought that she's right and you are hopeless.
- *Indirect* – Use emotional blackmail. If she wants to have continued contact with you, her child and grandchildren, she might want to think about what she says and does in your house.
  Alternatively you could create an atmosphere by telling her how pleased you are to see her and, of course, you'll cope with all the extra work.
- *Assertive* – Explain how you feel upset and undermined by her comments. Understand that it may be difficult for her to visit you and try to work out what would make it better for both of you. Work out ways that you can take care of yourself and not get wound up by her behaviour.

It's your turn to have your teenage stepson to stay for Christmas. You have been invited to a good friend's for Christmas dinner. They are happy to have your stepson but you know he will make rude remarks, rude noises and generally be unpleasant. You can't leave him alone on Christmas Day:

- *Aggressive* – Tell your stepson in no uncertain terms that one wrong step and he'll be sitting in your car for the afternoon.
- *Passive* – Beg your stepson to behave and offer to pay him well. Prepare to apologize for him and make excuses for his appalling behaviour.
- *Indirect* – Tell him how bad the repercussions of his misbehaviour would be. You can already feel a migraine starting at the thought of it.
- *Assertive* – Ask him for his help to make this a pleasant day for all of you, knowing he may feel awkward in a stranger's house. Find out if there will be anyone else there who's his age and, if not, whether there is a friend he could take along or be with for dinner-time.

If you decide not to visit your friend, be clear that this is an informed decision of your choosing and prepare to enjoy the day.

Professionals/public

Your doctor makes a dismissive comment when you ask her to explain the medication she is prescribing:

- *Aggressive* – Get off your snotty high horse for once and explain what you're giving me and why. Who do you think you are? How dare you dismiss me like a stupid child!
- *Passive* – OK. Thanks.
- *Indirect* – If you had any skill as a doctor you might just realize that you're the one talking mumbo jumbo, not me. Sorry I'm not as smart as you, but if you could find the time to tell me what you're poisoning me with I'd be grateful.
- *Assertive* – I know this is simple stuff to you, and it's complicated for me. I want to understand what it is you're giving me. I'd appreciate it if you could tell me what it does and why you're giving it to me. (When you use the word 'and' instead of 'but' it changes the meaning of the sentence quite significantly. Try it. When you say 'but' you discount what went before. When you say 'and' you are acknowledging and then adding to it. It may seem strange at first and it becomes easier.)

Your child's teacher asks you to go in and talk about your child's disruptive behaviour:

- *Aggressive* – You go prepared for a fight and accuse the teachers of not being in control (like they were when you were at school). This is before the teacher has had a chance to speak.

- *Passive* – You apologize profusely for your child's behaviour and agree that it isn't good enough. You say as little as possible, with no eye contact. You just want to run away.
- *Indirect* – Remind the teacher that you are friendly with the chair of the governors. Talk to other parents about the inefficiency of this particular teacher and how you all should get together and have him removed.

  Agree to the teacher's face, apologize, and then laugh with your child about it when you get home.
- *Assertive* – Listen to the teacher's comments and decide to ask your child for her account of things. Discuss options with the teacher and request a meeting with the three of you once you have had time to talk to your child.

Work

Without consulting you first, your manager has volunteered you to help a new member of another team write a company report:

- *Aggressive* – Tell your manager that she has behaved totally unreasonably and that you'd expect someone in their position to be more respectful. Just because she is your manager doesn't give her the right to arrange your diary.
- *Passive* – Worry how you will fit it all in. Resign yourself to taking more work home and not going out at the weekend as planned. Once at home, give your family a hard time handing out the aggression you daren't give your manager or you are feeling about your own lack of assertion.
- *Indirect* – Tell the person you're helping that this is just typical of your manager, who obviously doesn't understand the concept of consideration and respect for others. In fact, the new member of staff is lucky that they don't directly work with your manager.
- *Assertive* – Tell your manager how you feel about the situation and understand why she did it. Explain the impact the extra work will have and decide together how to prioritize your work. Bring the conversation round to working jointly on this not happening again. Help the other person as best you can within your work limits.

A member of your staff gives a good presentation to the rest of the department. They have worried about it for weeks:

- *Aggressive* – Applaud grudgingly and then bring the focus back on to you by changing the topic.

- *Passive* – Comment on how you could never be as good as him and how much you admire his courage.
- *Indirect* – Tell him it should have been good, considering how long he took to put it together. Suggest he might want to return to the rest of his work if he can cope with the mundane.
- *Assertive* – Congratulate him genuinely, appreciate the effort he put into it. Pick some specific examples of what made it good to enhance his appreciation too.

Each time I write the assertive example it strikes me how simple and straightforward it can be. We have to understand that when we are feeling on top of things and confident, we can handle anything that comes our way without panic. We are able to make clear requests and to set limits in a way that is respectful both to ourselves and to others. When we feel like this we consider the assertive behaviour perfectly normal and don't even think about it. It's when we're under pressure that we can tend to flip into the other behaviours.

Remember, assertive behaviour does not guarantee that you get what you want all the time. It means that the chances of getting to the best solution with everyone's self-esteem intact are greatly enhanced.

The table on the next page summarizes the four types of behaviours.

Once you have started to notice the way you behave and the options you have, you may find you are analysing other people's behaviours, too. It can be very frustrating when they don't respond the way you want, or they don't seem to understand you.

Change now

The whole thing about assertiveness is that you can handle non-assertive behaviour in a different way than you might have habitually done in the past. The trick is not to join in the other person's behaviour, but to stay calm and try to get your point across as you understand theirs. Sometimes we get caught up in their behaviour and the relationship declines. If you're the boss and someone is having a go at you, by becoming caught up in the argument you might feel the need to let them know that you're in charge, you're right and we're not having a discussion about this. Or you meet somebody behaving passively and you both end up saying, 'Ooh, well, I don't know, what do you think?' and by the time you've come to a decision the moment will have passed. If you tell someone that you don't like all the sarcastic comments they make about you and they suggest you loosen up and be able to take a joke, you may well want to have a go back at them and give them a sample of their kind of 'jokes'. Instead, acknowledge that it may have been meant as a joke, but affirm it's something you take seriously.

	Assertive	Aggressive	Passive	Indirect
Behaviour	Clear, calm, positive, RESPECT for both parties, can compromise	Shout, scream, swear, poke, hit, force, demand	Apologize, often say yes when mean no, 'agree', offer no opinion	Sarcastic, gossips, false flattery
You are	Able to set realistic limits, sincere and honest with self and others	Often unaware of the effect you have	Helpless victim, frustrated with self, unable to take responsibility	Self-critical and find fault with others, deny feelings, manipulative
Other feels	Acknow-ledged, listened to, valued, important	Threatened, frightened, anxious, angry/ furious, humiliated	Frustrated, unclear, powerful	Confused, guilty, wary, suspicious
Effects	Both involved in solution, work together, open communi-cations	Aggression back, no-one listens, avoidance, left alone, job done with fear, not co-operation	Self-anger can explode into aggression briefly, people stop asking your views, overtired, stressed and resentful	Others detect undercurrent of disapproval, worry what you're saying about them

Behaviour tips

Whichever behaviour you encounter, consider why the other person is behaving in that non-assertive manner. What is the information they are trying to give you and what do they mean to say? Ask yourself, 'How can I react to them in a constructive way and not passively, aggressively or indirectly?' You need to understand that, underneath the non-assertive behaviour, they're trying to tell you something that matters to them. You want to find a way of removing the layers in which they've 'dressed it up' to uncover the true message. If you can behave assertively and be honest about what's going on for you, then eventually they will come round to thinking, 'Maybe we can have a discussion about this.' If they have no serious message and are wanting to wind you up in some way (though of course this is a message, too), they will give up soon enough if you don't rise to the bait.

1 *Prepare positively*

Remind yourself that you have the right to make a request, refuse an offer or state your opinions. Use your positive self talk from Shift 5 and set yourself up for success. If all doesn't go completely to plan, then be ready to acknowledge what did work and what you might do differently next time.

2 *Be specific*

Decide what you want from a situation. Often we are so clear about what we don't want or don't like that it can take a little time to realize what our aim actually is. If you don't know what you want, how can anyone else? Leave them in no doubt about your position, in such a way that they feel able to disclose theirs, too. Think about using short, clear sentences that avoid waffle, hints or accusations. It is a good idea to be as specific as you can in anything you say. So if you want to give someone some feedback, describe precise behaviours, words, diagrams, times or places so there is no room for ambiguity or incorrect assumptions.

3 *Take a step back*

Sometimes we respond to people in one of our habitually non-assertive ways because we've been caught off balance or feel pressured to come up with an instant response to a complex question. The more you practise asking for time to think, or for information, the more likely you are to feel that you have regained some control and that you can give a considered response. By taking time to think about what is being said, you are much more likely to give a realistic and relevant response. The alternative may mean that you agree to something immediately, only to change your mind later on or take an inappropriate course of action that leads you into greater trouble further on down the line.

4 Recognize how you feel

It's important for you to consider how you feel in any given situation. It is also important to think: 'Am I going to share this feeling?' Sometimes people say, 'I feel quite frightened about the discussion that I'm going to have. I'm very wary of this person, but I don't want to tell them how I feel because then they'll get the upper hand.' There may be occasions when you decide not to disclose your feelings, and that's fine as long as you acknowledge them to yourself. Suppressed feelings are the cause of many misunderstandings and damaged relationships. When you express them their power is lessened and you can go on to discuss what it is you want to say.

5 Stick to your point

Repeat the phrase you want the other person to hear and avoid being hooked or side-tracked. If they are not keen to hear what you have to say they may, consciously or unconsciously, try to divert the discussion away from your original topic. Stay calm and bring them back. Take care, because a positive beginning can degenerate into an aggressive outburst or passive submission.

6 Empathize and understand

If you just keep repeating your phrase like an offensive parrot, you may worsen the situation rather than improve the relationship. You need to find a way of saying, 'I understand that you are concerned about x, and for now I would really like to clear up the issue of y.' If appropriate you could agree another occasion on which to sort out the 'x' issue. This will indicate that you know there is another issue and now is not the time for it.

7 Compromise

Negotiate from an equal position. When you compromise you leave both parties feeling good and as if there is something in it for them. It is important to realize that compromising on a solution need not compromise your self-respect, nor does it mean that they have won and you have lost. It means that you have both been able to move away from your first position to one that you both can accept. On those occasions where you don't feel able to compromise, find a way of agreeing to disagree without needing the other party to reach your conclusion.

8 *Relax and remember to breathe!*

If you ever watch someone who is very tense or feeling pressured, you will notice that their breathing becomes very quick and shallow. Think ahead and slow your breathing down so that there is a good flow of oxygen around your lungs and your head is clear. You will feel much calmer and more able to listen and consider before responding. The more relaxed you feel, the more in charge of yourself you can become.

Practise all of these tips as often as you can and you will be surprised how easy they become. Eventually they will be second nature to you and you will have some new habitual responding that serves you very well.

Shift 7

Increase prosperity through small change

Prosperity or lack of it is an outer expression of the ideas in your head.
(Hay, 1988)

If you have reached this Shift after reading all the preceding ones, then you will understand that your prosperity has already increased since Shift 1. You will have recognized how to reach your goals and what might have prevented you from doing so previously. From Shift 3 you will have cleared plenty of physical and emotional space, leaving room for lots more 'goodies' to enter your life. You will have a 'success log' in which to record all the good things that occur on a daily basis, and you will be feeling more positive about yourself in many ways. Prosperity is, simply, plenty of everything. It is something we create inside us, rather than something we acquire externally.

When I started thinking about the content of this Shift, it became clear to me that wealth and prosperity are much wider concepts than just money. Even if you have started by reading this Shift first you can consider extending your notion of wealth beyond purely monetary value. You will still be wealthier than you first thought. There are many aspects to prosperity and abundance; material wealth is only one component. You could also consider:

- good emotional, mental and physical health;
- fulfilling relationships;
- energy and enthusiasm for life;
- creative freedom;
- being appreciated and valued;
- nurturing friendships;
- freedom of speech and mobility;
- enjoying the natural beauty of flowers, trees, birds and butterflies;
- a sense of well-being and peace of mind;
- Add more of your own indicators of wealth _____

_____

_____

_____

_____

70

Prosperity audit

Think back to Shift 1, when I encouraged you to consider the goals in various aspects of life. I wonder whether any of them included a notion of worth and prosperity? Take some time and use a table like the one below to work out how you would describe prosperity and wealth in each area that applies to you.

For example, you may consider in the category 'living space' that having a room to yourself, whether that be a bedroom, study room, hobby room or eating room, would constitute a high level of prosperity. Or in 'contribution' you may feel that you could give more of your time or skills for the benefit of a local group.

A score of 1 means you are low on satisfaction and control in that category, a 10 means that you have reached the level at which you feel entirely satisfied and empowered.

	What constitutes wealth or prosperity?	Where am I – 1–10?	How to get higher?
Social life			
Relationships			
Family			
Finances			
Work			
Living space	Own room to relax	3	Start with corner of a room and gradually spread – with agreement
Leisure			
Health			
Retirement			
Spiritual life			
Contribution	Involved with school	3	Find out about PTA, governors, school trips
New habits or releasing old ones			
Personal development			

Nolli met her new partner at a mutual friend's house. She enjoyed his company and felt very attracted to him. She had always thought that any long-term relationship would be with someone 'in work'. She was surprised how much she enjoyed her first summer with Nazim and didn't need any financial input from him. She felt she had found a partner who nurtured her in such a way that she was healthy, wealthy and well provided for. He gave her more than money could buy.

Prosperity is the state of mind that creates money and pleasure in our lives.

(Carson and Lawson, 1990)

You can't simply measure it by counting your possessions or amounts in the bank. It relates to your attitude towards yourself and the world around you. Prosperous people enjoy their lives and use their 'moments of choice' in a positive way. They have time to notice and experience everything that is going on around them, rather than getting stuck in the one thing that isn't right. They feel comfortable acknowledging and meeting their needs and recognize abundance in its broadest sense.

Question

What are you worth? What do you deserve?

I can think of times when I haven't asked for a reasonable pay rise or taken money for something I've made because I think, 'It's not worth it.' What I have learnt is to then substitute the 'It's' with an 'I'm'. When I say, 'I'm not worth it' the sentence takes on a different meaning and I question whether I am in some way lowering my self-esteem and putting myself down. There is also an important distinction when offering something as a gift or donation. I choose to donate my time, creativity or expertise, because I want to. I am acknowledging my worth and giving it for free and freely.

Prosperity begins with feeling good about yourself and being open to the many possibilities that are available to you. It is not an amount of money as much as a state of mind. Sometimes we are so convinced that we do not deserve wealth or success or that we are unworthy. Then we sabotage ourselves from getting what we want. If we don't believe we are worthy, and abundance comes our way, then we somehow reject it. So if we get some spare cash from somewhere, we instantly spend it so as to return our normal state of being broke. We don't acknowledge the extra because it's not a part of our perception of ourselves.

If you believe that you can only achieve anything worthwhile through hard work, then it will always be a struggle. If, on the other hand, you believe that prosperity is easy to come by, then it will be. You give yourself the freedom to respond to whatever life throws at you rather than being straitjacketed in the 'shoulds' and 'oughts'. Once something is considered to be 'hard work', it immediately creates a heaviness and pressure of its own. Some people are scared by the possibility that good things can just come their way, and only remember the experiences which confirm that things don't go well for them. I recognize this when I hear people say things like, 'If anything can go wrong, it will do,' or 'Nothing good ever comes my way.'

> Trudy is stuck in her 'bad luck' trap when she says, 'Of course, it's all right for you, you can think positively about things. It doesn't work for me and I always lose out.' Read that sentence again: what is she saying to herself?

We know that what we think is what we get, and so she creates her own limiting reality. She is unable to take the risk of trusting in herself and her world because she subconsciously believes that she is meant to suffer in her life. Gradually she is starting to listen to her needs, taking a few risks and surviving. And yes, it probably does seem OK for me. I am a lot more comfortable with myself than I used to be and I believe that I deserve a life that I enjoy and value. I also know that I have the choice to sit and wallow some days, and how to pull myself out of it when necessary.

I remember some years ago when I had a very bad back. I was almost bent double with the pain. I experimented with a variety of therapies and different practitioners to try and sort it out. Eventually I was talking to a good friend who suggested a local sports injuries specialist. I was horrified. 'Have you any idea how much he charges?' was my main concern. She simply said to me, 'How much are you and your back worth?' What a fabulous question! In fact, she could even have asked me, 'How can you afford not to go to him?' I knew then that I owed it to myself and those around me to find a way to meet his fees and recover. That was a most important learning for me. I could find a way to afford his treatment and he set me on my way to health and fitness. Without his intervention I would have spent many more months disabled and struggling to make ends meet.

I learnt well from my friend, and unashamedly ask the same question of people I work with now – what is your health, happiness, quality of life, worth?

You can find ways of increasing your self-worth by just asking, 'Am I worth it?' and respond 'Yes, yes, yes.' It may be in giving yourself the gift of time or the opportunity to read, take a walk, a long bath or a run, rather than always subsuming your needs in other people's. Don't feel guilty. Feel proud that you care enough about yourself to know you matter. Make sure that you have plenty of entries in your rewards bank.

Folklore

In Shift 2 – 'Who says you should?' – you considered the rules that were part of your family's history. Some were positive permissions that encouraged your learning and growth. Others were injunctions which, although given with good intent, had the effect of holding you back. There are many family and society sayings which relate to money, its use, its effect and its origins.

'Money is the root of all evil.' A fascinating saying, especially as it has been corrupted from the original form in the Bible which says, 'The love of money is the root of all evil.' Quite a different notion. I wonder when the phrase was distorted and for whose benefit. Clearly the first statement is nonsense. How can money be the root of all evil? It is a crucial part of the bartering system that we all use and recognize. It is an ancient, accepted and recognized means of creating opportunities for everyone to meet their needs and benefit from the utilizing of all their different skills and abilities. You don't work for money *per se*, but for what money can buy. The love of it, to the exclusion of anything else, is another matter. There are people who are fabulously wealthy and don't seem to reap any joy or benefit from it. They are too busy either counting and hoarding their fortunes or working all the hours to amass more so that their collection is ever growing. They have lost sight of the wealth from relationships with people and the natural world.

Question

What are the sayings you associate with wealth and money?

In Shift 4 – 'What are you telling yourself?' – we consider the effect that your thoughts have on your feelings and your subsequent actions. This is also true in your relationship with and thoughts about money and abundance.

Take a moment or two to think about the sayings relating to money that you heard as a child and still say to yourself. List them down or record them on tape. Go through them and use different colours or different voice tones to distinguish those that are positive and those that are limiting. Notice the feelings and actions that accompany each one. Using the table below, make a new list with all the positive, encouraging ones and create some contradictory and uplifting affirmations for the ones that restrict you.

Saying	Positive and keep	Negative and replace
I am open to receive abundance from expected and unexpected sources.	I am open to receive abundance from expected and unexpected sources.	
There is plenty for everyone.	There is plenty for everyone.	
Money doesn't grow on trees.		Money is made of paper, paper is made from wood. Hooray, money grows on trees!
All things come to those who wait.		Abundance comes effortlessly into my life.

Notice how you feel about money and your worthiness when you use the positive affirmations. Make up as many as you want and factor in some time to be able to enjoy the results. There are many stories and cautionary tales to warn us away from greed and avarice. It seems to me that they emanate from a suspicious and scared mentality. If we are able to trust ourselves and others and believe that there is enough for everyone, this may radically alter our approach to life.

Greed stems from fear of lack, not fear of money.

Go with the flow

The word 'affluence' is derived from the Latin verb meaning 'to flow towards'. It is helpful to think about money as part of the natural movement of energy in the world. If you consider money a symbol of life energy, then you will appreciate the need to keep it moving. If you stop its circulation by hoarding or holding it back, you will also stop it flowing back into your life. Like a river, money must keep flowing, otherwise it begins to stagnate, clog, suffocate and strangle its very own life force. The saying 'What goes around comes around' certainly applies here. If you think about the way money moves in your life, you may become aware of a rhythm or ebb and flow that is uniquely yours. Perhaps there is a pattern over a month or a year that coincides with the way you relate to money.

For you to create a state of wealth consciousness, it is crucial that you are able to release your attachment to whatever you want. Attachment is based on fear and insecurity which stifles your ability to be creative. The more you try to hold on to something or somebody, the more likely you are to lose them. Attachment to money creates insecurity no matter how much you have in the bank. Some of the people with the most money in the bank are the most insecure, because they are afraid of losing it and having to live life without it.

Question

Do you spend your money freely and with pleasure?

Some people feel restricted in the way that they spend their and other people's money. (Though some are rather more generous with the latter!) Even 'hard-earned' cash is sometimes held on to because we feel guilty about spending it on exactly what we want. This may stem from lack of self-worth again, or from popular, judgemental stories of vulgar consumerism and ostentation. The concepts of spoilt children and being born with a silver spoon in your mouth serve only to stop us valuing and spoiling ourselves. Just to be sure that we are not offending others, we hold ourselves back.

The notion of 'poverty consciousness' suggests that if you always look for the cheapest item on the menu, or buy a cheaper item of clothing when you can afford and would prefer something more expensive, you are focusing on lack rather than abundance. You will obviously make choices about how you spend whatever money you have; the key is to enjoy giving yourself the best you can. Spending your money creates a flow of energy which enables everyone to benefit. You feel pleased to have something you want and feel good about. The sales assistant has earned their commission and the manufacturer has made some profit with which to pay their employees. They then have enough money to put back into circulation, which will benefit you directly or indirectly. 'Money is like muck, not good except it be spread' is the way Francis Bacon describes the necessary flow. If you collect muck it simply stagnates and smells; if you spread it around it fertilizes and stimulates growth.

Check out whether you are stingy with yourself, and if so think about changing and moving out of poverty consciousness. Maybe buy fewer, more expensive items and thoroughly enjoy them, rather than 'economizing' and wishing you hadn't settled for second best. Start to focus on what is available to you and create some helpful affirmations like:

- I deserve the best that is available to me and I am willing to pay for it.
- It is safe for me to spend my money on meeting my needs.
- I enjoy spending my money.
- I always have enough money.

> Whatever we don't use, we lose.
> (Matthews, 1999)

This applies to our physical bodies, our skills and our money. If you break an arm and it is in plaster for a long time, it becomes weak and less effective. Your money muscles also need to be used and exercised. Successful business people reinvest their capital using what they have and taking calculated risks. Your money is not going to grow if you keep it in a biscuit tin under the bed.

Paolo was offered the chance to stay rent free in a house in California. He had never been abroad and was thrilled at the prospect. His challenge was how to fund the travel for himself and his teenage children. He had some money saved in the bank but didn't want to spend it, just in case ... We talked about his fears of 'blowing it all' on a whim, rather than having it in reserve. We also discussed what he and his family were worth. His money was doing nothing in the bank, and wouldn't it be a shame if he died with it still there and untouched? On the other hand, if an emergency arose he would know that the money was there to cover it. On the other hand, this opportunity may not be available again and he could start to save up and get the children involved in money-making schemes. On the other hand . . .

Which choice would you make, and why? Whichever it is, make it and then get on with the rest of your life. Resist the temptation to regret and wonder what might have been. Rather than fix yourself firmly at one or other end of the spectrum, work out a balance of spending and saving that works for you. One of my colleagues decided to collect any £2 coins that she had. She quickly amassed enough for a great day out with the family.

Moment of choice

You can choose whether to have a scarcity mentality or an abundance mentality.

If you choose a scarcity mentality, you will want to hold on to what you have, 'just in case'. Your thinking will be focused around your ability to acquire from what seems to be a finite and limited pot. You will struggle to celebrate other people's successes because that would detract from you, as if they are taking something from you with their special recognition or outstanding success. Their success could be perceived as your failure. You're always competing and comparing, and your self-worth stems from possessing things or power over others. You need to keep looking over your shoulder to make sure your possessions are safe. You only want to know 'what's in it for me?' If there isn't enough to go round, you need to hold on to what you've got. If you think in terms of 'filthy rich' you will keep yourself poor – you wouldn't want to associate with people you despise.

To have an abundance mentality, you believe there is plenty for everyone and more than enough to go round. From a position of deep self-worth and inner confidence you are able to share in others' successes and give freely. Your giving enables and empowers you, too. You are able to feel good about other people being prosperous. You don't have to struggle keeping things to yourself and secretly working on your own. You are free to express yourself in whatever way feels good. Others will appreciate and value your openness and honesty. You are aware of participating in a world full of beauty and focus on what you have rather than what you might lack. You can train yourself to pay attention to the joys inherent in your everyday experiences. Notice the stars on a clear evening, smile at the birdsong in the park, enjoy a hug with a close friend. Relish being alive and appreciate what you have. Whatever you concentrate on increases. Choose to focus on the many aspects of your abundance and immediately increase your riches.

Give it away

Become a giver and enjoy the rewards of understanding and reaching out to someone else. Move out of your world and think about what is happening in theirs. This is one of the most powerful ways to give because you are focusing on what they need from their perspective, rather than what you think will be 'good' for them. Give regularly to your favourite charity. One of the best ways of feeling good about money is to give some of it away, especially to a person or deserving cause that needs it even more than you do. Be sure you donate your gifts sincerely and with gladness, otherwise the gesture becomes meaningless.

Giving generates receiving, and this all contributes to the continuing flow of energy. It may not result in a swollen bank balance, but more a deep sense of happiness, peace and health which are not necessarily available to someone merely rich in money. Wealth that is shared creates more wealth, and you can share many forms of wealth besides money.

Every year we take part in a pantomime organized locally. We, the performers, give our time to rehearse and our fabulous talent to entertain. A dedicated wordsmith and songwriter provide our raw materials. The props team come to most rehearsals and make many of the marvellous items that we wield in every scene. The scenery and backcloths are so skilfully painted that the locations are three-dimensional and you can imagine looking out through the painted windows. The prompt says more than most on the first night and has to keep in touch with all the changes made to the script right up to the first performance. A mass of volunteers come out in force to erect a stage, run the bar, sell the tickets and supervise the audience. Talented electricians work the lights and sound effects and a very versatile pianist accompanies the songs and fills in while the sets are being changed. Make-up is bought and supplied, and a very small team creates wonderful colourful costumes to set the whole production alight. The audience freely give their laughter, applause and occasionally sympathy. The end result is a wonderful sense of community, and we all share the recognition and appreciation for our varied contributions.

Give some of your wealth away and see what happens.

Question

Are you able to receive prosperity with pleasure?

Strange though it may seem, compliments are gifts of prosperity which some people struggle to accept. They either reject them – 'What, this old thing?' or 'It was nothing special' when they have put lots of energy into something – or they hand them back without even registering them – 'But you always know what to say' or 'Your writing is much better than mine.' The giver can feel rejected and eventually stop. Practise accepting compliments graciously and enjoying someone else's recognition and appreciation.

Peace of mind

Peace of mind has been called 'the wealth without which you cannot be really wealthy' (Hill, 1998). If you are comfortable with yourself, you increase the possibility of bringing wealth into your life. You are in the habit of thinking in terms of what you want to do rather than the obstacles in the way. You are in the habit of giving before trying to get. With peace of mind you can live your life on your own terms, in values of your own choosing, so that every day your life grows richer and greater.

It would be unrealistic of me to suggest that there is no need for money to assist in creating peace of mind. If you don't know where the next meal is coming from or whether you can keep a roof over your head, you are unlikely to have peace of mind. Having said that, if the main purpose of a fortune is to make the owner worry about holding on to their money, peace of mind cannot endure here either. Sufficient money is necessary to almost everyone who wishes to attain peace of mind. How much is something only you can answer. Use the affirmations and exercises in this Shift to reach the amounts you want.

Imagine

Start by concentrating on your breathing and allow yourself to relax into your chair or on the floor if you are lying down.

Enjoy the thought that you are going to release any tension and know that you deserve the time you are giving yourself.

Relax and breathe slowly.

With your breathing, allow your body to settle and relax.

Imagine yourself in a place that is warm, safe and

welcoming to you. This could be indoors, outdoors, on land or on water, on earth or on another planet.

A place designed to meet all your needs and fulfil all your expectations.

Look around you. Take in the beauty and wonder that surround you. Enjoy the intensity of the colours you can see.

Marvel at the harmony and melody of sounds.

Experience deep and joyous feelings of peace and calm.

RELAX.

Every sense is filled with a positive message. Let it be and let it envelop you. This is your space, your place, that you can create and go to any time you choose. Somewhere to open yourself to yourself and take in all your positive thoughts.

Now imagine yourself being where you want to be in your life and being the person you want to be. Enjoy the sounds, sights, smells, tastes and feelings that accompany this state. As you notice how much more you can achieve, relax, and allow your subconscious to help you make the choices that support and nourish you.

When you are ready, return to the place you are in, knowing you can visit your space any time you want to or need somewhere comfortable and relaxing to collect your thoughts. Be ready to open your eyes, feeling great and inspired, ready and able to create and live in the world you desire.

From now on you can start to take greater control of your life. Act as if you have already achieved many of your goals and appreciate feeling a greater sense of direction. Live it, practise it and believe it. You have made some positive shifts in your thinking. Enjoy the change.

You have to leave the city of your comfort and go unto the wilderness of your intuition. What you'll discover will be wonderful. What you'll discover will be yourself.

(Alan Alda, actor)

Further reading

Black, Jack, *Mindstore*, Thorsons, 1992

Branden, Nathaniel, *The Six Pillars of Self-Esteem*, Bantam, 1995

Burns, Dr David, *Feeling Good*, Avon Books, 1992

Carson, Justin, and Lawson, David, *Money and Your Life*, Healing Workshops Press, 1990

Chopra, Deepak, *The Seven Spiritual Laws of Success, A Practical Guide to the Fulfilment of Your Dreams*, Bantam, 1996

Covey, Stephen R., *The Seven Habits of Highly Effective People*, Simon and Schuster, 1999

Dyer, Wayne, *Everyday Wisdom*, Hay House, 1993

Hay, Louise, *You Can Heal Your Life*, Hay House, 1988

Hill, Napoleon, *Grow Rich with Peace of Mind*, Piatkus, 1998

Holland, Stephanie, and Ward, Clare, *Assertiveness: A Practical Approach*, Winslow Press, 1990

Jeffers, Dr Susan, *Feel the Fear and Do It Anyway*, Rider, 1997

Jeffers, Dr Susan, *Feel the Fear . . . and Beyond*, Rider, 1998

Kingston, Karen, *Clear Your Clutter with Feng Shui*, Piatkus, 1998

Lawson, David, *I See Myself in Perfect Health*, Thorsons, 1995

Matthews, Andrew, *Being Happy! A Handbook to Greater Confidence and Security*, Media Masters, 1999

Mulligan, Eileen, *Life Coaching, Change Your Life in Seven Days*, Piatkus, 1999

Quilliam, Susan, *Stop Arguing, Start Talking*, Vermillion, 1998

Robbins, Anthony, *Awaken the Giant Within*, Simon and Schuster, 1992

Roet, Dr Brian, *The Confidence to be Yourself*, Piatkus, 2000

Shapiro, Mo, *Understanding Neuro-Linguistic Programming in a Week*, Institute of Management and Hodder and Stoughton, 1999

Silva, Jose, and Goldman, Burt, *The Silva Mind Control Method of Mental Dynamics*, Grafton, 1990

Taylor, Ros, *Transform Yourself*, Kogan Page, 2000

Contact the author

Mo Shapiro offers one-to-one coaching sessions and *Shift Your Thinking, Change Your Life* workshops. She is available for corporate speaking and training engagements, along with writing for additional print publications.

Visit the website: www.inform-global.com
Or e-mail Mo on moshapiro@inform-global.com
Or write to her via Sheldon Press, 1 Marylebone Road, London NW1 4DU

Index